INSPIRED
JEWELRY

INSPIRED JEWELRY

From the Museum of Arts and Design

Ursula Ilse-Neuman

John Bigelow Taylor and Dianne Dubler, Photography

Museum of Arts and Design, New York, in association with ACC Editions, Woodbridge, England, 2009

museum of arts and design

Two Columbus Circle
New York, NY 10019
212-299-7777
www.madmuseum.org

ACC EDITIONS

ACC Editions is an imprint of
Antique Collectors' Club Ltd.
Sandy Lane, Old Martlesham
Woodbridge, Suffolk IP12 4SD, UK
www.antiquecollectorsclub.com

Project Coordinator: Jennifer Scanlan, Museum of Arts and Design, New York
Editor: Nancy Preu, Orono, Minnesota
Designer: Paola Gallerani, Officina Libraria, Milan
Layout: Agata Maja Żurkiewicz, Officina Libraria, Milan
Color separation: Antique Collectors' Club, Woodbridge, Suffolk and Eurofotolit, Cernusco sul Naviglio (Milan)
Printed in China

Photographs for *Inspired Jewelry* are by John Bigelow Taylor and Dianne Dubler with the following exceptions:
Bally, p. 228: Ed Watkins; Bennett, p. 84: Ed Watkins; Bennett, p. 85: John Lenz; Cavalan, p. 146: Richard Goodbody; Corvaja, p. 185: Maggie Nimkin; Friedlich, p. 208: James Beards; Jünger, p. 86: Ed Watkins; Knobel, p. 130: Martin Tŭma; Metcalf, p. 6: Ed Watkins; Nijland, p. 209: Eddo Hartmann; Petry, p. 231: Christian Brown; Pomodoro, p. 46: Ed Watkins; Ramshaw, p. 147: Bob Cramp; Sherman, p. 211: Kevin Sprague; Slemmons, p. 201: Maggie Nimkin; Strzelec, p. 198: Book Leidy; Vigna, p. 222: Moscheni-Lorenzi; Wang, p. 199: Cherry Kim; Wiener, p. 64: Eva Heyd; Woell, p. 57: Eva Heyd

Frontispiece
Boris Bally (United States, 1961–current residence, United States) | *Arachnid Armform* · 1986 | silver, goldplate, rubber bands, metal springs | 4 $^1/_2$ x 4 $^1/_2$ x 4 $^1/_4$ in. (11.4 x 11.4 x 10.8 cm) | gift of the artist, 1995
Page 6
Bruce Metcalf (United States, 1949–) | *Pin #28* · 1988 | gold leaf, enamel paint, maple, brass | 5 x 3 $^3/_4$ x $^3/_4$ in. (12.7 x 9.5 x 1.9 cm) | gift of Helen Williams Drutt English, 2008
Page 8
Tina Rath (United States, 1968–) | detail of *Belgian Floral Collar* · 2000 | see p. 216

CONTENTS

FOREWORD

The Museum of Arts and Design is pleased to present *Inspired Jewelry*, a book of exceptional pieces of art jewelry from our internationally renowned collection.

Since its inception in 1956, the Museum has been committed to contemporary jewelry. Our focus in our exhibitions and publications has been on the astounding mastery of materials and techniques through which art jewelers translate their visions into reality. The dividend of our effort is that people the world over now experience this vibrant art form with new eyes and a deeper understanding.

This volume celebrates the opening of the Museum's new home on Columbus Circle and the inauguration of the Tiffany & Co. Foundation Jewelry Gallery, where our entire jewelry collection is on view for the first time. With a permanently open window on this rapidly evolving art form, and with our collection accessible through an extensive database, we anticipate sharing our excitement for jewelry with a growing number of enthusiasts.

Numerous artists and collectors around the world have helped to establish MAD's collection as one of the finest internationally, and we are grateful to all of them for their dedication and generosity. We particularly would like to acknowledge several gifts that have been important in shaping the character of the jewelry collection: in the 1950s, works acquired from the American Craft Council first brought the collection to a critical mass; in 1969, a major gift from the Johnson Wax Corporation greatly enriched the holdings in both scope and depth; and in recent years, substantial gifts from Sandy Grotta, Donna Schneier, Barbara Tober, Nanette Laitman, and Marcia Docter have carried the collection into the twenty-first century.

We are extremely grateful to a number of individuals who made this project possible. First and foremost, we extend our appreciation for the contribution of MAD Curator Ursula Ilse-Neuman, whose extensive knowledge of jewelry and whose dedication to the Museum are reflected in the growth of the collection during her tenure. My gratitude also goes to Chief Curator David McFadden, whose personal vision has greatly strengthened MAD's collection and its exhibitions program. Thanks as well to Jennifer Scanlan, associate curator, who coordinated the publication of this volume, and to Sara Mandel and Maya Jimenez, curatorial assistants, who prevailed over endless details with patience and perseverance. Photographers John Bigelow Taylor and Dianne Dubler deserve special mention: it was their captivating images of our jewelry collection that first caught the eye of publisher Marco Jellinek. Final recognition is reserved for Dorothy Globus for her inaugural installation of the Museum's jewelry collection and Nancy Preu for her keen editorial eye.

Finally, I extend my deepest appreciation to the Board of Trustees for supporting this exhibition and publication and, above all, to the Tiffany & Co. Foundation for its exceptionally generous contribution. Through our exciting new jewelry gallery and our flourishing publication and exhibition program, we look forward to encouraging ever greater appreciation for contemporary jewelry.

Holly Hotchner, Director
Museum of Arts and Design

INSPIRED JEWELRY

Contemporary jewelry, like many art forms today, is expanding its boundaries. Even as most jewelry artists continue to create works that relate in size, shape, and weight to the human form, others probe the limits of wearability and indeed the very nature of jewelry and its role in contemporary culture.

Art jewelry is highly refined and technically accomplished, yet it is created to satisfy the deeply embedded, if not irrational, human impulse to decorate the body, an impulse that can be traced back tens of thousands of years to the earliest known jewelry forms. Contemporary jewelry embodies a complex and dynamic balance of opposing forces—the sophisticated and the instinctive, the traditional and the innovative, the personal and the social, the cool and the hot—that makes it one of today's most vital art forms.

* * *

The Museum of Arts and Design's jewelry collection was started in 1958, two years after the establishment of the institution as the Museum of Contemporary Crafts. The earliest works in the collection date from the late 1940s, when the vast amount of energy that went into the arts following World War II created a revolution across many media. In jewelry, which has always been a barometer of society, the radical changes in the postwar landscape gave rise to a new and enduring art form that is known today as studio, or art, jewelry. Rejecting mass production and traditional jewelry's reliance on gemstones and precious metals, pioneering artists/craftsmen extolled the value of works made by one individual, from concept to execution, and sought out new sources of inspiration, primarily in the fine arts.

The acceptance of jewelry as art was fostered in the United States very quickly after the war by major museums such as the Museum of Modern Art in New York and the Walker Art Center in Minneapolis. In 1946 the landmark MoMA exhibition *Modern Jewelry Design* brought together the "artist as jeweler" and "jeweler as artist" by showing jewelry by painters and sculptors such as Alexander Calder, Harry Bertoia, and Jacques Lipchitz alongside works by jewelry makers such as Sam Kramer and Paul Lobel. Beginning in 1948, the Walker Art Center organized a series of exhibitions entitled *Jewelry for Under $50.*

Over the last sixty years, diversity has been the one constant in jewelry design as artists have explored a range of approaches, supplementing established goldsmithing traditions with unconventional materials and innovative techniques. Rapid globalization is further enriching the vocabulary of the international jewelry community as Western and non-Western imagery and ideas circulate among artists in contemporary jewelry centers that are now spread around the globe, from Europe to Australia and from the United States to Japan, Korea, and beyond.

In this essay, attention is focused on the principal ideas that have inspired the unique jewelry in the Museum's collection. Broadly speaking, these works reflect the wide range of concerns that have informed creative expression in the visual arts over the last six decades.

MODERNIST JEWELRY

In the 1930s, New York City became the epicenter of the avant-garde in America. The Beat Movement thrived in the cafes of Greenwich Village, an extraordinary community of artists, writers, musicians, filmmakers, and actors. After World War II, the Village became a stronghold for pioneering jewelers who were inspired by the twentieth-century art movements of Constructivism, Cubism, Surrealism, Biomorphism, and the New York School of Abstract Expressionist painting.

Rejecting the prevailing decorative jewelry styles that depended on precious metals and stones, these Modernist jewelers conceived their pieces as fine art to wear and established their shops as small galleries. The most memorable character on the Greenwich Village jewelry scene was Sam Kramer (1913–1964), whose studio/shop advertised "Fantastic Jewelry for People Who Are Slightly Mad," and whose designs featured biomorphic amoebic shapes inspired by Surrealism. In his *Necklace* and *Earrings* from the 1940s (pp. 24 and 25), Kramer used molten metal to create free-form shapes that emerged from his subconscious, in much the same manner that the Abstract Expressionists applied paint to their canvases.

When Art Smith set up his jewelry workshop in Greenwich Village in 1946, he was one of a very few African Americans working in the field. As opposed to the majority of jewelers of his time, who focused primarily on brooches, pins, and rings, Smith created extravagant neckpieces and bracelets that displayed his awareness of the body as a living armature. Among the many devotees of Smith's jewelry were members of New York dance and theater companies who thrilled to the way his dramatic designs came to life when worn. The Museum's 1948 *Neckpiece* (p, 23) in hand-hammered brass is elegantly shaped in biomorphic contours and exemplifies Smith's theatrical approach.

Other important New York City artists in the collection who were influenced by Biomorphism include Ed Wiener and Paul Lobel. In reaction to the inferior quality of costume jewelry, Paul Lobel designed inexpensive jewelry in sterling silver and gracefully bent wire, emphasizing simple and recognizable forms such as the violin in his *Stradivarius* brooch produced in his Greenwich Village studio around 1945 (p. 27). Ed Wiener believed that an artist must chronicle the artistic trends of his time. His work evolved over the years in response to the major trends in modern art. This is evident in comparing his sterling silver biomorphic *Pin* (p. 26) from 1949–52 with his 1966 *Opal Brooch* (p. 64) suggesting the two-dimensional, formalist approach of the color-field painters in the 1960s and also reflecting the use of opulent gemstones in Asian jewelry, with which he became familiar during his travels in India.

While many sculptors made jewelry principally as a diversion, Abstract Expressionist Ibram Lassaw took a serious approach to the one-of-a-kind objects for the body that he called Bosom Sculptures. The Museum is fortunate to have his 1972 *Neckpiece* (p. 75) featuring an array of interlocking right-angle elements in gold-plated bronze.

On the West Coast, Margaret De Patta was one of the most important and influential jewelers of the postwar era. Conceptually and technically, her forms were highly sophisticated, reflecting the Constructivist principles she learned from former Bauhaus master Lazslo Moholy-Nagy at the School of Design in Chicago, where she studied from 1940 to 1941. Following Moholy-Nagy's advice to "catch" her stones in the air ("Don't enclose them. Make them float."), De Patta devised methods for holding stones without bezels or prongs. The illusion of unsupported, floating river stones is evident in the *Pin* she created between 1960 and 1964 (p. 42).

Responding to Moholy-Nagy's interest in light and space, De Patta was excited by the possibilities of creating optical and visual effects in clear quartz stones by making innovative lapidary cuts (which she called opti-cuts) to exploit internal reflections and refractions that change with the wearer's movement. The effects of her experimentation can be admired in her 1946 quartz and onyx *Ring* (p. 29) and in her exceptional crystal and diamond *Pendant* from 1960 (p. 43).

When De Patta formed the San Francisco Metal Arts Guild in 1951, she was joined by Bob Winston, who is represented in the Museum's collection by his 1969 cast gold *Ring* (p. 61); Irena Brynner, whose 1967 gold *Earrings* (p. 59) exemplify her use of the lost-wax casting technique; and Merry Renk, who also studied in Chicago with Moholy-Nagy, and who is represented in the collection by her stunning 1968 *Wedding Crown* (p. 44).

From the 1950s on, stylistic and technical advances taking place in Europe exerted an important influence on design in many media, including jewelry. The Scandinavian Modern design aesthetic introduced by Nordic silversmiths and industrial designers, in particular, had a profound impact on metalwork and jewelry. This is evident in Henning Koppel's 1958 sterling silver *Bracelet #287* (p. 33) for Georg Jensen, the renowned Danish silversmith firm. In the ensuing decades, exhibitions and lectures by visiting European jewelers were also crucial, notably those by Hermann Jünger, a master German goldsmith whose career as artist and teacher spanned more than five decades. Jünger developed new artistic and technical approaches that allowed him to translate the freedom and fluidity of his drawings into jewelry. His success at making these transformations can be seen by comparing his gold and enamel *Halsschmuck* neck ornament from around 1980, one of his finest works, with his exquisite working drawing for this piece (pp. 86 and 87).

SCULPTURAL JEWELRY

Many of the artists in the collection are attracted to the sculptural aspects of jewelry and the challenge of balancing form and mass in space on an intimate scale. Included in this group are artists whose shapes and structures are related to the principles of architecture and engineering, as well as those who create organic abstractions from nature and those who assume a minimalist approach that shuns ornament or figuration.

Inspired by Architecture and Engineering
In the last sixty years, developments in architecture and engineering have altered the environment as well as the way we connect with one another and our world. Jewelry artists who are attracted to

compositions underscoring structure, balance, volume, and space often draw on principles borrowed from engineering and architecture and employ industrial materials not conventionally associated with jewelry. Works like Eva Eisler's 1990 stainless steel and silver *Brooch* from her Tension series (p. 152) convey a sense of equilibrium that stems from her fascination with the engineering of intricate structures such as bridges. Eisler admires the beauty of their physical construction as well as the metaphor they offer for connecting one thing to another. Excellent examples of the technical virtuosity of constructing interrelated elements include Stefano Marchetti's 2002 gold *Bracelet* (p. 182), Sergey Jivetin's 2004 brooch *Intersection* (p. 189), composed of hundreds of tiny watch hands, and Tamiko Kawata's 2006 neckpiece *Black Orpheus* (p. 191), built with a myriad of interlocking safety pins. In his 2003 *Brooch* (p. 183), Peter Skubic exploits the reflective qualities of lacquer and stainless steel, as well as the contrasts between these two components, in a complex spatial composition. Other artists project an industrial aesthetic, including David Tisdale in his anodized aluminum *Disk Bracelet* from 1982 (p. 96) and Zack Peabody in his 1994 *Brooch #528* (p. 155), which connects stainless steel and plated brass with braided wire and threaded nuts.

David Watkins and Wendy Ramshaw, husband and wife, have been prolific and influential jewelers for more than forty years. The collection follows the career-span of these two British artists with over eighty of their works, including Watkins's technically demanding 1984–85 *Voyager* neckpiece (p. 100) in neoprene-coated wood and steel. In this complex composition, repetitive elements are layered to form a multidimensional structure, perhaps reflecting the new perspectives he gained designing models for Stanley Kubrick's film *2001, A Space Odyssey.* For her 1988–89 *Orbit Necklace & Earrings* (p. 97), Ramshaw was inspired by space age design, deliberately balancing the bold, mechanistic patterns of nickel alloy inlaid with black resin with movable discs that "orbit" around the wearer's neck as if in a solar system of their own. In her *Set of Six Ring Stands & Rings* from 1981 (pp. 98–99), Ramshaw integrates yellow and white gold rings with nickel alloy stands resembling space ships.

Inspired by Organic Forms
The use of natural structures as a springboard for the creation of beautiful or thought-provoking body ornament involves distillation of the essential from the particular. In contrast to the "precision engineering" of much of the jewelry in the Museum's collection, the organic forms are animated by subtle undulations in shape, color, and line. Using diverse materials, from the woven gold in Mary Lee Hu's 2002 *Bracelet #62* (p. 186) to the cut and stained wood in Liv Blåvarp's 2002 *Necklace* (p. 219) to the sensous, carved ivory of Pavel Opočenský's 1986 *Brooch* (p. 105), these artists translate natural contours into jewelry attuned to the body.

Inspired by Minimalism
Groundbreaking developments in jewelry took place in the Netherlands in the late 1960s when a diverse group of goldsmiths and designers led by Gijs Bakker and his wife Emmy van Leersum removed extraneous ornament and used nonprecious materials to establish a new form of jewelry that was independent of associations with wealth or social status.

With the introduction of such pointedly nonprecious materials as aluminum, steel, rubber, plastic, and paper, the new Dutch style was democratic—that is, affordable and accessible—and became known as Dutch Smooth. Minimalist, yet eye-catching and flamboyant, Dutch Smooth works include dramatic sculptural neck collars and head decorations such as van Leersum's 1969–70 *Bracelet* (p. 50) and Bakker and van Leersum's collaborative 1967 *Armband* (p. 51).

Timeless works that follow in the Minimalist tradition include Lisa Gralnick's 1988 black acrylic *Bracelet* (*Cube*) (pp. 94 and 95) and Lella Vignelli's folded sterling silver neckpiece *Seicento* from 2003 (p. 202). Thomas Gentille's 1991 circular *Pin* in synthetic resin inlaid with pigment (p. 151) is abstract and cerebral with careful regard for formal relationships and subtle color combinations.

Conceptual Jewelry

Taking Minimalism to its limit, in 1973 Gijs Bakker made a gold wire that was to be twisted tightly around the arm to make an imprint on the skin. When the wire was taken off, the mark it left became "shadow" jewelry. What interested Bakker more than the jewelry itself was its effect on the body. The fact that there was no tangible end product that could be worn alienated some people, but he made his point by exhibiting the wire in a silk-cushioned box, accompanied by a photograph of the imprint on the skin.

The purpose of jewelry, the experience of wearing and owning it, and the morality of materialism are still hotly debated topics, yet jewelry that comments on these issues is rare. However, someone who has been successfully creating jewelry that does just that for over twenty years is Swiss-born Otto Künzli, a keen and iconoclastic commentator on the meaning of jewelry in our society. He is well represented in the collection with six works that draw attention to the "blind" acceptance of conventions. A case in point is his celebrated *Gold Makes You Blind* bracelet from 1980 (p. 93), an icon of twentieth-century jewelry in which a black rubber tube completely shrouds what is assumed to be a gold ball. The wearer must take on faith that the gold is there, while the artist questions the reliance on preciousness in valuing jewelry. In his 1980 *Ring for Two* (p. 92), two steel rings are connected by a bar, locking two wearers together through one piece of jewelry. The steel symbolizes the strength and endurance of the commitment that binds the couple and comments on the social role of jewelry beyond its ornamental function.

PAINTERLY JEWELRY

While form and composition are fundamental to all jewelry, some artists give paramount importance to color and texture, making the surface of the object their canvas. The techniques they employ include staining, painting, enameling, inlaying of metals or other materials, granulation, and the incorporation of colorful stones, plastics, and glass.

Inspired by Color

Trained as a painter, Earl Pardon reinvigorated ancient cloisonné enameling in American studio jewelry. In his 1989 *Necklace* (p. 83), Pardon created intricate enameled collages with subtly different combinations so that each plaque acts as an individual painting. Marilyn Druin's 1998 *Egyptian* necklace (p. 144) is a superb example of the *basse taille* enameling technique, which features sensuously textured surfaces created by shallow etching and roller printing the metal surface and then applying multiple layers of transparent and translucent enamel.

William Harper's masterful and innovative enameling approach is well represented by his 1979 *Transfigured Mystery* (p. 73) brooch. Combining enameling with gold, silver, a baroque pearl, and a plastic bicycle reflector, the piece is a triumphant demonstration of Harper's mastery of color and his ability to create an intricate composition through the juxtaposition of various materials, patterns, lines, and shapes. Harper's 1995 *Shove Causes a Push* neckpiece (p. 145) was created in honor of a legendary 1976 ballet by noted choreographer Twyla Tharp. In this piece, colorful enamel elements rotate on neck wires, suggesting the movement of the dancers.

In his *Aiuola Brooch #19* from 1988 (p. 85), Jamie Bennett uses an enameling technique he invented in which an electroformed structural base produces muted colors and matte finishes. Annamaria Zanella creates a striking counterpoint of color using oxidized silver, gold, and enameling to emulate bold gestural brushstrokes in her 2002 brooch *Building* (p. 190).

Over the centuries, artists have capitalized on the mineralogical patterns and luster of colorful stones to create vibrant tones and textures in their jewelry. The Museum's collection features many excellent examples of such work, including the 1960s silver and turquoise *Bracelet* of Native American Charles Loloma (p. 65). In an intriguing blend of traditional Navajo designs and modern abstraction, Kim Rawdin paints with stones in his stunning bracelet *How Many Wine Cups Have Stained This Moon with the Songs of Old Friends* from around 1997 (p. 162). Other striking examples are the asymmetrical contrast of gold and lapis lazuli in Bernd Munsteiner's *Brooch/Pendant* of 2001 (p. 224) and Rami Abboud's fantastic conglomeration of gold, topaz, tourmalines, sapphires, and diamonds in *Omnipotent* ring from 2007 (p. 220).

Acrylic, a durable and moldable twentieth-century material available in a wide range of brilliant colors, is well suited to making jewelry. Peter Chang pioneered its use and acceptance in his eye-catching *Bracelet* of 1985 (p. 89), working tiny acrylic fragments into brilliant multi-layered patterns in a celebration of plastic's mutability and color.

Inspired by Texture

Many jewelry artists generate interest by devising intricate surface textures. Two timeless examples from Italy include Gio Pomodoro's 1963 *Brooch* in white and yellow gold, which features deep crevices and cracks resembling a volcanic landscape (p. 47). An interesting contrast is the cloudlike surface texture in Giovanni Corvaja's gold and platinum *Brooch* (p. 185), made forty years later, in 2003. Tone Vigeland's sensuous 2000 *Bracelet* (p. 193) brings a monochromatic array of steel beads together into a meshlike tube to form a kinetic field of texture that sways and moves with the body. Stanley Lechtzin's *Brooch #68B* from 1967 (p. 48) was made using the electroforming technique he pioneered to create thick but feather-light impasto texture in silver gilt.

NARRATIVE JEWELRY

From earliest times, artists have told stories through their creations. Whether depicting their messages on the walls of ancient caves, portraying mythological scenes, or recounting the history of civilization or their personal lives, artists have communicated through pictures or potent symbols. Similarly, contemporary jewelry artists speak to us through stories relevant to our time and create forms and images that possess iconic value today.

Inspired by Signs and Symbols

Some of today's studio jewelry is spiritually linked to the talismans and amulets of the earliest known jewelry. Sam Kramer's 1958 *Roc Pendant* (p. 37), with its fabulous mythological creature casting a symbolically charged eye on all who look his way, has the quality of an amulet. Ramona Solberg combined objects she regarded as talismans—a bit of Alaskan ivory, a silver fish, a small figure, an old coin—into the 1968 *Shaman's Necklace* (p. 66), whose title refers to Northwest Coast Native American spiritual healers. Dylan Poblano challenges the stereotype of "American Indian jewelry" in order to transform tradition for a new generation. His *21st-century Neckpiece* from 2001 (p. 207) assembles a chaotic assortment of found and constructed components in silver and quartz into a complex composition that functions in multiple ways. Its removable parts include earrings, rings, a pin, and a pendant, each of which can be worn separately.

Few artists are as profoundly involved with the mystical aspects of jewelry as Dutch jeweler Ruudt Peters. His fiery red *Iosis Pendant and Brooch* of 2002 (p. 196) was created when he first became interested in alchemy, and his intention was that it represent excitement and passion as well as shame and injury.

Another aspect of narrative art is the use of text and language to provide visual and structural elements. The shapes and outlines of characters in languages such as Hebrew, Arabic, and Chinese are often used by contemporary artists independently from their actual meaning. Robert Ebendorf, artist and teacher for over forty years, deserves special mention. His use of found objects has been enormously influential, justifying his view that anything can be made into jewelry. In his 1985 *Neckpiece* (p. 90) and his 1988 *Collar* (p. 91), Ebendorf incorporates Chinese newspaper. The script in these neckpieces is exploited for visual impact, with no regard for meaning, as opposed to the Chinese characters in Kee-ho Yuen's 1995 *Brooch* (p. 172). In her 2000 *Thread of Faith* neckpiece (p. 204), Alyssa Dee Krauss strings rusty letters on a thin gold thread to suggest that her poem about a princess being carried off by a prince is only a vanishing dream. Kiff Slemmons considers her *Nibs* necklace from 2000 (p. 205), with its silver pen nibs and fragments of old handwritten manuscripts framed under mica, to be an homage to writing. The imagery of modern-day emblems and their associations were central to Pop Art. Verena Sieber-Fuchs's comical *Head Jewelry* of 1986 (p. 122) incorporates an image of Mickey Mouse, one of the most recognizable icons of American pop culture, and pokes fun at the rodent's dual status as a symbol of goodwill and a symbol of corporate hegemony. Wilhelm Tasso Mattar was looking for a colorful material as a substitute for enamel and chose the packaging components from two world-famous consumer products to create his *Coca-Cola Nivea Necklace* in 1982 (p. 110).

Inspired by Social and Political Issues

Jewelry artists have been remarkably ingenious in expressing their views about the environment, social injustice, consumerism, and the human condition. Their approach can be sharply humorous, poignant, or disturbing as they produce wearable forms that attract the eye and challenge the mind.

J. Fred Woell is credited with being one of the first American jewelers to use jewelry for outspoken politically and socially relevant work. His *The Good Guys* pendant from 1966 (p. 57), one of the highlights of the collection, uses the images of comic strip heroes as icons to reflect the cultural and political turmoil that spawned the 1960s counterculture. In his 1998 *"Borghese" Brooch* (p. 138), Gijs Bakker sets a laminated photograph of Renaissance *putti* atop a silver soccer ball. By conflating iconic images from religion and sports, Bakker makes a biting, albeit playful, commentary on the "religious" character of sports in popular culture.

At once critical and hopeful, African American jewelry artist Joyce Scott sees gender, race, and class as traps that can be escaped by challenging accepted beliefs and institutions. In her vibrant *Voices* neckpiece of 1993 (p. 175), Scott created closemouthed beaded faces using a unique African American quilting technique, the peyote stitch, to string the beads together. Verena Sieber-Fuchs protests social injustice in her 1988 *Apart-heid* collar (p. 119) by incorporating tissue paper used by South African workers for wrapping fruit. Boris Bally takes aim at gun violence and hip-hop bling by assembling his 2006 *Brave #2* neckpiece (p. 229) from one hundred actual handgun triggers.

Nancy Worden's 1994 neckpiece *The Seven Deadly Sins* (pp. 168 and 169) is very much in the tradition of social commentary as Worden deflates celebrities of an earlier era through the clever use of such familiar objects as Hershey Kisses wrappers, machine screws, and a credit card fragment. Gluttony is linked to the older Elvis Presley; Greed to Imelda Marcos, the profligate wife of the late Philippine president Ferdinand Marcos; and Lust to Woody Allen for his well-publicized escapades. Instead of focusing on broad social issues, some jewelers focus on the plight of the individual amidst the stresses of contemporary life. Bruce Metcalf's expressive narrative figures are frequently faced with human dilemmas that become even sharper by being distilled into grotesquely humorous cartoons, as is the case in his brooch *Missing the Prison* from 1987 (p. 132). Gijs Bakker designed the silver *Liberty* brooch (p. 139) in 1997 for former United States Secretary of State Madeleine K. Albright. The brooch consists of two watches: one watch set upside down to allow her to keep track of time during her interviews; the other, right side up to show her visitor when it is time to leave.

Siberian Necklace #1 from 2007 (p. 227) is one of Ted Noten's eighteen "portraits" of stops along a lengthy train journey from Tokyo to the Netherlands, made from objects as diverse as grasshoppers and cultured pearls that he acquired along the way. In her *It's About Time* neckpiece from 2005 (p. 188), Laurie Hall assembled clock works to form a gate commemorating the defining moment in her artistic life when she met jeweler Ramona Solberg, her mentor.

INSPIRED BY THE NATURAL WORLD

The inclusion of representations of plants, animals, and other natural objects has a long tradition in jewelry. In contrast to jewelry inspired by organic forms, these works are more literally rendered and some even incorporate actual natural materials. Examples include the rose petals in Carrie Garrott's 2004 *Cluster Brooches* (p. 214) and the butterfly wings and peacock feathers in Jennifer Trask's 2003 *Blue/Black Necklace* (p. 215).

Virtuosic granulation and enameling are employed to replicate the colors and textures of a sea polyp in John Paul Miller's 1969 *Armored Polyp* neckpiece (p. 62). David Freda is an ardent naturalist who spends endless hours bird watching and scuba diving in order to arrive at his finely wrought silver and enamel depictions of animals and flowers. His painstaking devotion to accuracy meshes with his compositional inventiveness and gives new life to such specimens as the delightful *Vagabond Butterfly Fish* in his neckpiece from 1985 (p. 104).

Natural flora expressed in colored glass are central to Linda MacNeil's elegant and meticulously formed jewelry. Her 2003 *Grandiflora Brooch* from the Flower series (p. 210) is based on her observations of flowers and branches. Sondra Sherman's *Corsage: Papaver Somniferum–Poppy* (2007) from her Anthophobia: Fear of Flowers series (p. 211) is shaped as a traditional corsage in steel covered with nail polish. The series includes medicinal herbs and alludes to our anxiety-provoking social system.

INSPIRED BY THE BODY

Body fragments, internal organs, and cell structures are some of the points of departure for artists inspired by the body to make jewelry for the body. One of the most stunning objects is Italian artist Bruno Martinazzi's 1992 *Metamorfosi* bracelet of the human hand (p. 141), an icon of twentieth-century art jewelry. Playing on the personalization of certain parts of the body—the nose, heel, or fingers—Gerd Rothmann uses his own palm as the central motif in his *Palm Print* bracelet of 1997 (p. 143).

Internal body structures are the subject of English artist Dorothy Hogg's elegant but disquieting portrayal of blood vessels in her 2005 *Large Circle Neckpiece* from the Artery series (p. 200). Julia Barello emphasizes human frailty and vulnerability by making the inner workings of the body visible. Her 1996 *Vascular Studies II: Lung* brooch (p. 142) is modeled from her own vein and artery patterns and is displayed when it is not being worn on an X-ray of her lungs installed in a lightbox.

INSPIRED BY PERFORMANCE ART

Beginning in the 1970s in Great Britain and Holland, the body became the foundation for wearable forms that blurred the distinction between jewelry, clothing, and performance art. Jewelers who distinguished themselves through the use of fiber included Caroline Broadhead, who wanted to make jewelry that would dominate, rather than accentuate, the body. Disdaining the need to make jewelry comfortable and practical, she extended jewelry's range in such works as her 1982 *Sleeve 4* (p. 113) and her 1983 *Veil* (p. 112).

Susanna Heron's 1977 *Jubilee Neckpiece* (p. 71) was also influential in removing the distinction between jewelry and clothing and in testing the boundaries of wearability—to the extent that wearing the piece was often interpreted as a "happening." Another contributor was Lam de Wolf, whose

1983 oversized construction for the body, *Yellow Shoulder and Body Piece* (p. 120), was designed to empower the wearer and change established attitudes about jewelry. More recently, in 2002, Japanese artist Emiko Suo challenged the wearer to become the center of attention through her outlandishly-sized *Collar* (p. 195) in stainless steel, gold, and silver leaf.

Along more wearable, but no less pioneering, lines, Arline Fisch played a prominent role in expanding the boundaries of jewelry in the 1960s through her application of textile techniques to metal and also through dramatic, large-scale body sculptures such as her 1966 *Body Ornament* (p. 52) made of forged sterling silver.

Marjorie Schick has followed a uniquely independent course in exploring new sculptural jewelry forms that extend into the space around the body. Positioned at the nexus of jewelry making, sculpture, and performance art, Schick is best known for her complex dowel-stick constructions of the 1980s. The Museum's dramatic *Collar* from 1988 (p. 127) radiates a concept of jewelry that goes well beyond the conventional boundaries of form, materials, and color.

INSPIRED BY TECHNOLOGY

In the latter half of the twentieth century, a number of jewelry artists looked to new technologies in their work. Vernon Reed's 1985 *Comet Zero* (p. 135) resulted from his belief that cybernetics and microelectronics provided a natural (r)evolutionary path for jewelry in the late twentieth century. Mary Ann Scherr's twelve-inch *Electronic Oxygen Belt Pendant* from 1974 (p. 77), with concealed electronic components and an oxygen mask, alludes to the fragility of life.

In the current electronic age when we perceive the world through digital imagery and virtual realities, the development of a new direction in jewelry design based on computer-aided design and computer-aided manufacturing (CAD/CAM) is a natural progression. With its dispassionate, high-tech appearance, CAD/CAM jewelry is a natural counterpart to the ubiquitous cell phone and iPod.

Under the guidance of Stanley Lechtzin, who pioneered using the microcomputer as a tool for studio jewelry in the 1980s, the epicenter of CAD/CAM jewelry is the Tyler School of Art in Philadelphia. Lechtzin's 1999 *Plus-Minus Brooch* (p. 177) and his wife Daniella Kerner's *Mag Brooch* of the same year (p. 176) have an otherworldly beauty reflecting their creation without the touch of the human hand.

The ease with which computers can produce and replicate a piece of jewelry raises the questions of whether such jewelry can take on the value of one-of-a-kind creations and whether jewelry produced by a computer artist is as significant as a piece that has been labored over by hand. Lechtzin suggests that every CAD/CAM work can be made unique by recalculating (and deleting) the control program. These authorship issues will be the subject of lively debate in the years ahead.

* * *

By its nature, jewelry is the art of extroversion. At its best, contemporary jewelry allows us to rejoice in the triumph of ideas realized through the transformation of remarkable materials and the execution of masterful techniques. Contemporary art jewelry is not a symbol of wealth and status but an enduring statement of personal affinities and discernments. When someone wears his "art on his sleeve," his passions, preferences, and even politics are revealed for all to see.

Ursula Ilse-Neuman, Curator
Museum of Arts and Design, New York

Dimensions of the jewelry on the following pages are cited as height x width x depth unless otherwise indicated.

Margaret De Patta

Art Smith

Sam Kramer

Ed Wiener

Paul Lobel

40s

Margaret De Patta (United States, 1903–1964)
Pin · **1947–50**

Silver, coral, malachite
2 $^7/_8$ x 3 $^1/_2$ x $^5/_{16}$ in. (7.3 x 8.9 x 0.8 cm)
Gift of Eugene Bielawski, The Margaret De Patta Bequest,
through the American Craft Council, 1976

Art Smith (United States, 1923–1982)
Neckpiece · **1948**

Brass
6 $^1/_2$ x 7 $^{11}/_{16}$ x 1 $^1/_2$ in. (16.5 x 19.5 x 3.8 cm)
Purchased by the American Craft Council, 1967

Sam Kramer (United States, 1913–1964)
Earrings · c. 1945

Silver, wire, garnet, jade
3 x 1 ³/₈ x ³/₄ in. (7.6 x 3.5 x 1.9 cm), each
Gift of Nina D. Fieldsteel, 1999

Sam Kramer (United States, 1913–1964)
Necklace · 1940s

Silver
8 ¹/₄ x 6 ³/₈ x ⁵/₈ in. (21 x 16.2 x 1.6 cm), overall
1 ¹/₂ x 2 ⁵/₈ x ¹/₄ in. (3.8 x 6.7 x 0.6 cm), pendant
Gift of Nina D. Fieldsteel, 1999

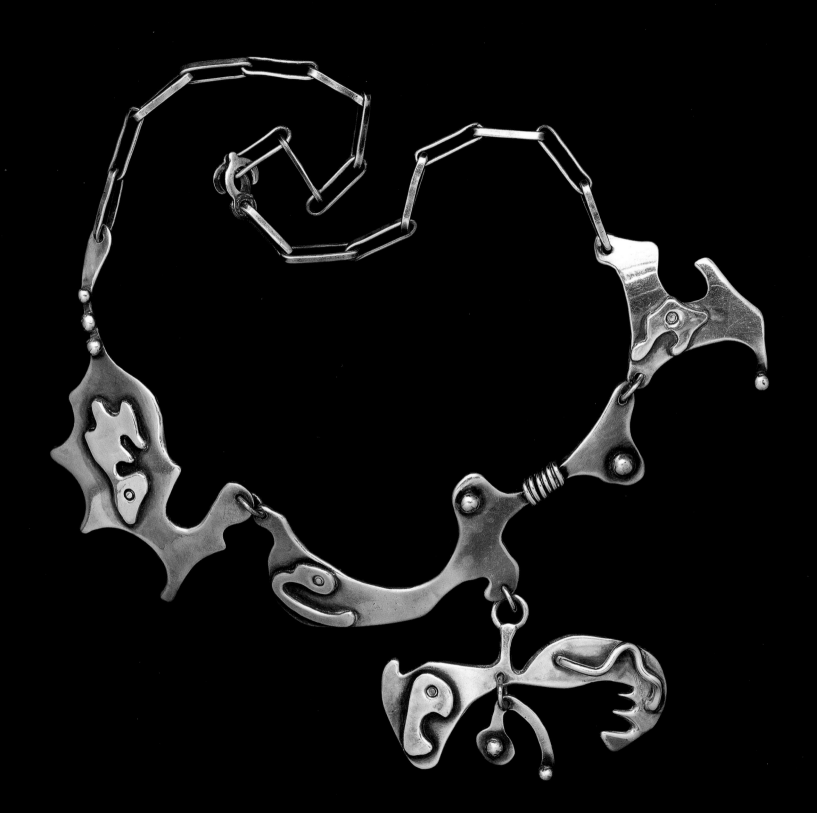

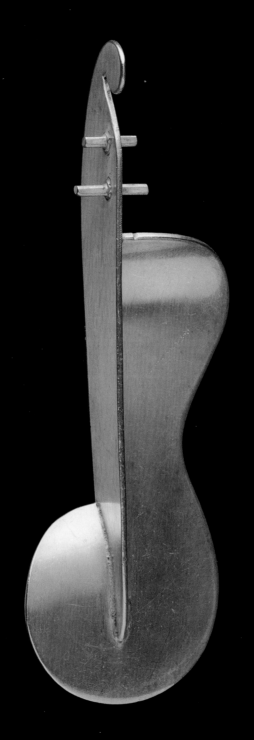

Paul Lobel (Romania, 1899–1983, United States)
Stradivarius **(brooch)** · **c. 1945**

Silver
4 ¼ x 1 ⅛ x ½ in. (10.8 x 2.9 x 1.3 cm)
Promised gift of Susan Grant Lewin, 2008

Margaret De Patta (United States, 1903–1964)
Ring · **1946**

Gold, rutilated quartz, black onyx
1 x ³⁄₄ x ³⁄₄ in. (2.5 x 1.9 x 1.9 cm)
Gift of Eugene Bielawski, The Margaret De Patta Bequest,
through the American Craft Council, 1976

Ed Wiener

Henning Koppel

Ronald Hayes Pearson

Betty Cooke

Margret Craver

Sam Kramer

Claire Falkenstein

50s

Ed Wiener (United States, 1918–1991)
Silver Brooch with Pearl · c. 1955

Silver, pearl
1 ³/₄ x 3 x ⁵/₈ in. (4.4 x 7.6 x 1.6 cm)
Gift of Michele Caplan, 1999

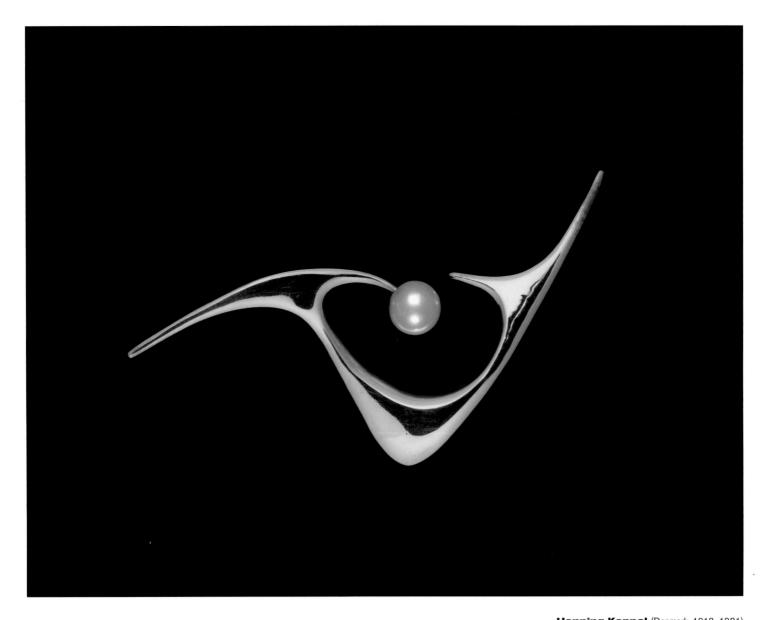

Henning Koppel (Denmark, 1918–1981)
for **Georg Jensen**, Copenhagen
Bracelet #287 · 1958

Silver
2 ¹/₂ x 2 ¹/₂ x 2 ¹/₈ in. (6.4 x 6.4 x 5.4 cm)
Gift of Amy Hanan, 2000

Ronald Hayes Pearson (United States, 1924–1996)
Necklace · c. 1959
Silver
5 ¹⁄₄ x 5 x ¹⁄₂ in. (13.3 x 12.7 x 1.3 cm)
Purchased by the American Craft Council, 1959

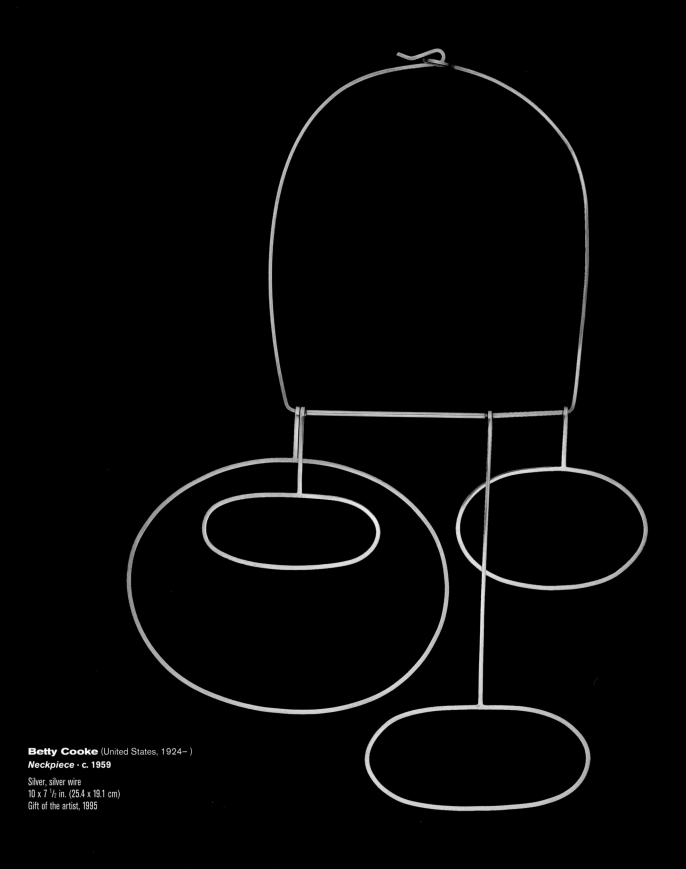

Betty Cooke (United States, 1924–)
Neckpiece · c. 1959

Silver, silver wire
10 x 7 ½ in. (25.4 x 19.1 cm)
Gift of the artist, 1995

Margret Craver (United States, 1907–)
Hair Ornament · **1959**

Gold, en résille enamel, gold foil
5 ³/₄ x 2 ³/₈ x ⁷/₈ in. (14.6 x 6 x 2.2 cm)
Commissioned by the American Craft Council, 1959

Sam Kramer (United States, 1913–1964)
Roc Pendant · **1958**

Silver, gold, ivory, horn, taxidermy eye, coral, tourmaline, garnet
4 ³/₄ x 2 ¹/₄ x ³/₄ in. (12.1 x 5.7 x 1.9 cm)
Purchased by the American Craft Council, 1967

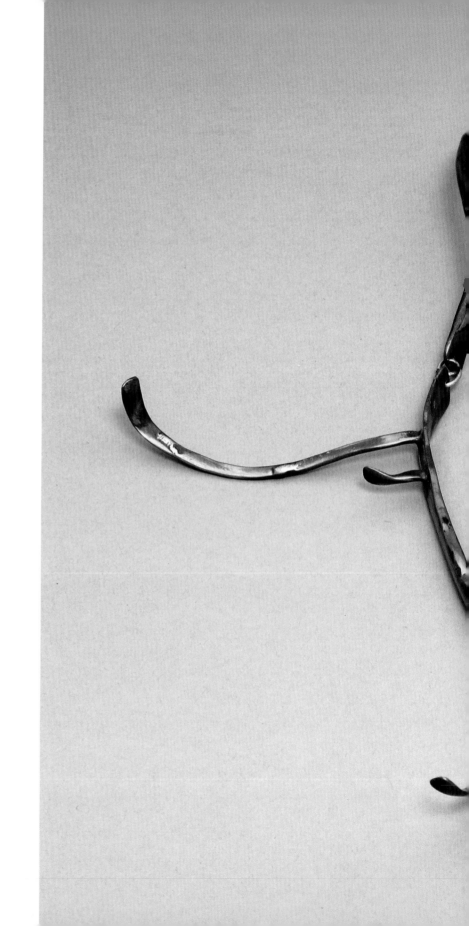

Claire Falkenstein (United States, 1908–1998)
Necklace · **1950s**

Copper
12 ³⁄₄ x 13 x 1 in. (32.4 x 33 x 2.5 cm)
Gift of Kim and Al Eiber, 2008

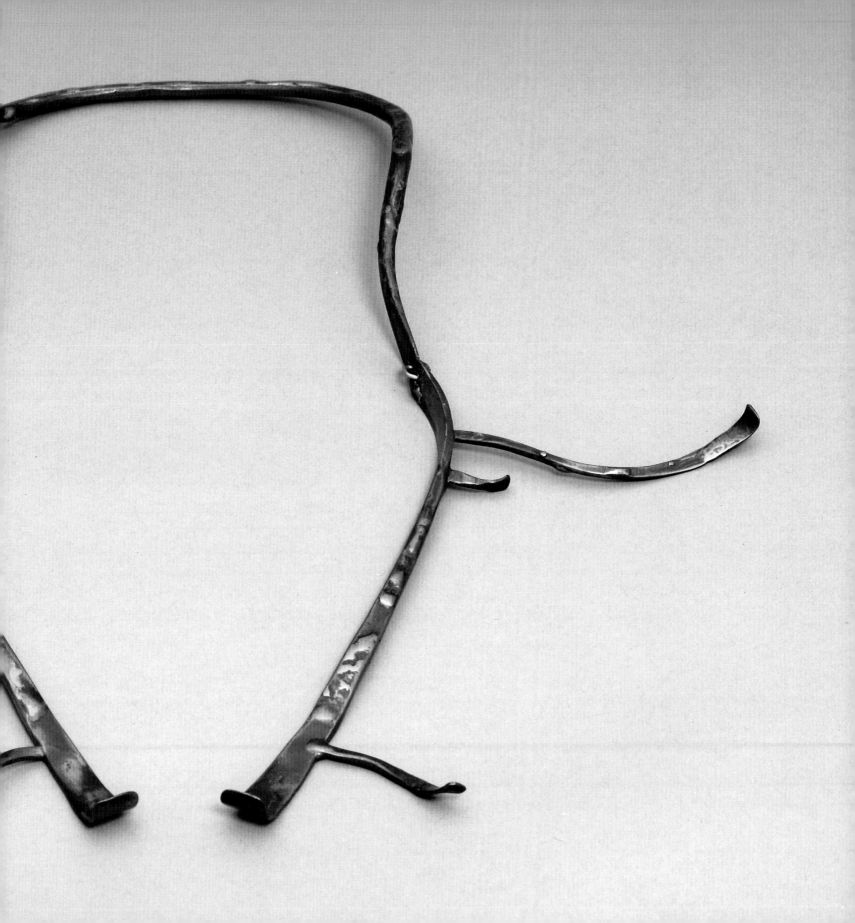

Margaret De Patta

Merry Renk

Gio Pomodoro

Stanley Lechtzin

Olaf Skoogfors

Emmy van Leersum

Gijs Bakker

Arline M. Fisch

Alma Eikerman

Art Smith

Vivianna Torun Bülow-Hübe

Ken Cory

J. Fred Woell

Phillip Fike

Irena Brynner

Joe Reyes Apodaca

Bob Winston

John Paul Miller

Ruth Radakovich

Ed Wiener

Charles Loloma

Ramona Solberg

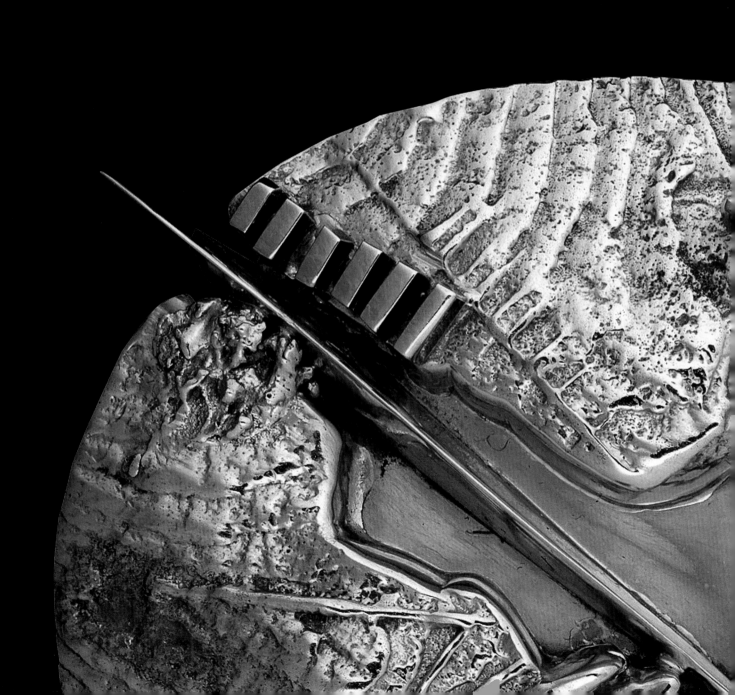

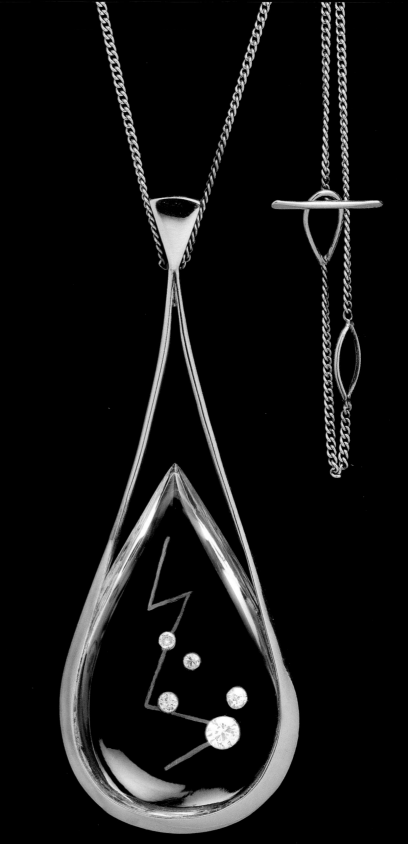

Margaret De Patta (United States, 1903–1964)
Pendant · **1960**

Crystal, diamonds, gold
9 ¹/₄ x 4 ³/₄ x ¹/₂ in. (23.5 x 12.1 x 1.3 cm), overall
3 x 1 ¹/₈ x ¹/₈ in. (7.6 x 2.9 x 0.3 cm), pendant
Gift of Eugene Bielawski, The Margaret De Patta Bequest,
through the American Craft Council, 1976

Merry Renk (United States, 1921–)
Wedding Crown · **1968**

Gold sheet, wire, cultured pearls
3 x 6 ¼ x 6 ¼ in. (7.6 x 15.9 x 15.9 cm)
Gift of the Johnson Wax Company, through the American Craft Council, 1977

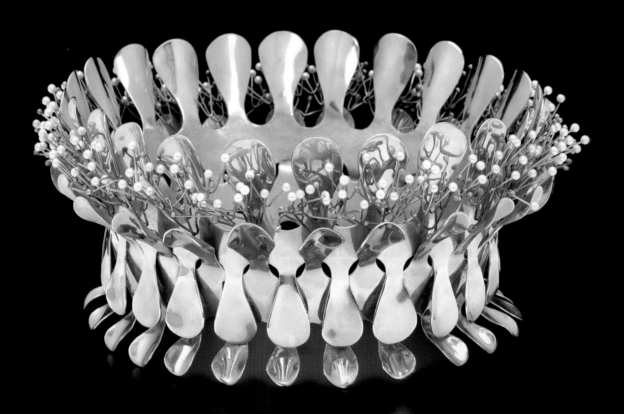

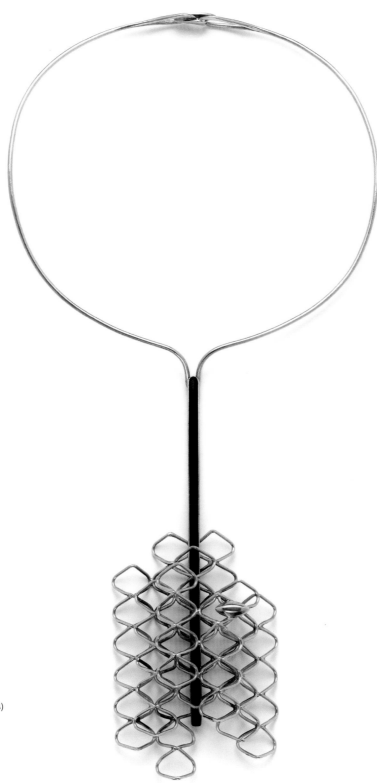

Margaret De Patta (United States, 1903–1964)
Pendant · 1961

Gold, ebony, wire
9 $\frac{1}{2}$ x 4 $\frac{3}{4}$ x $\frac{3}{4}$ in. (24.1 x 12.1 x 1.9 cm)
Gift of Eugene Bielawski, The Margaret De Patta Bequest,
through the American Craft Council, 1976

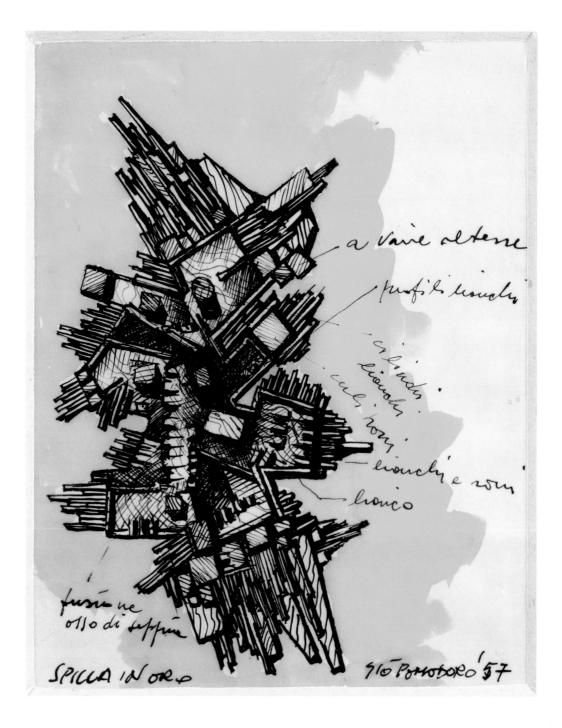

Gio Pomodoro (Italy, 1930–2002)
Studio per una Spilla in Oro [Study for a Gold Brooch] · 1957

Ink, gouache on paper
4 $^5/_{16}$ x 3 $^9/_{16}$ in. (11 x 9 cm)
Gift of Dorothy Twining Globus, 2005

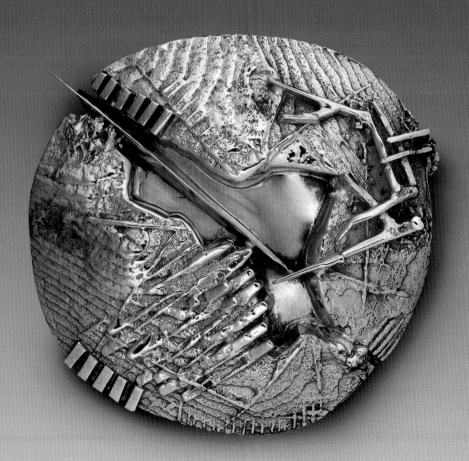

Gio Pomodoro (Italy, 1930–2002)
Brooch · 1963

Gold
2 x 2 ¼ x 2 in. (5.1 x 5.7 x 5.1 cm)
Museum purchase with funds provided by the Collections Committee, 2006

Stanley Lechtzin (United States, 1936–)
Brooch #68B · 1967

Silver gilt, tourmaline, crystal
3 ⅛ x 3 ¼ x 1 in. (7.9 x 8.3 x 2.6 cm)
Gift of Edith Lechtzin, through the American Craft Council, 1967

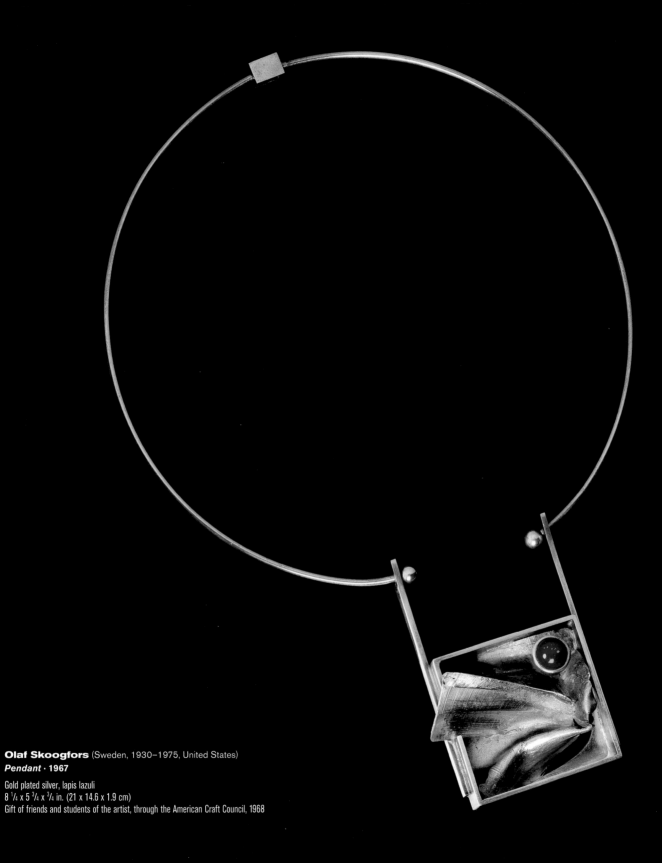

Olaf Skoogfors (Sweden, 1930–1975, United States)
Pendant · 1967

Gold plated silver, lapis lazuli
8 ¼ x 5 ¾ x ¾ in. (21 x 14.6 x 1.9 cm)
Gift of friends and students of the artist, through the American Craft Council, 1968

Emmy van Leersum (The Netherlands, 1930–1984)
Bracelet · **1969–70**

Steel
2 ⁵/₈ x 2 ¹/₂ in. (6.7 x 6.4 cm)
Gift of Donna Schneier, 1997

Gijs Bakker (The Netherlands, 1942–)
Emmy van Leersum (The Netherlands, 1930–1984)
Armband (bracelet) · **1967**

Aluminum
5 x 4 ¹/₄ x 1 ³/₄ in. (12.7 x 10.8 x 4.4 cm)
Gift of Donna Schneier, 1997

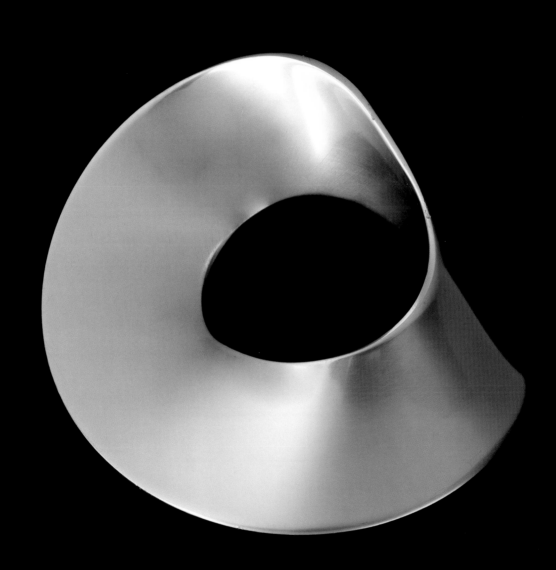

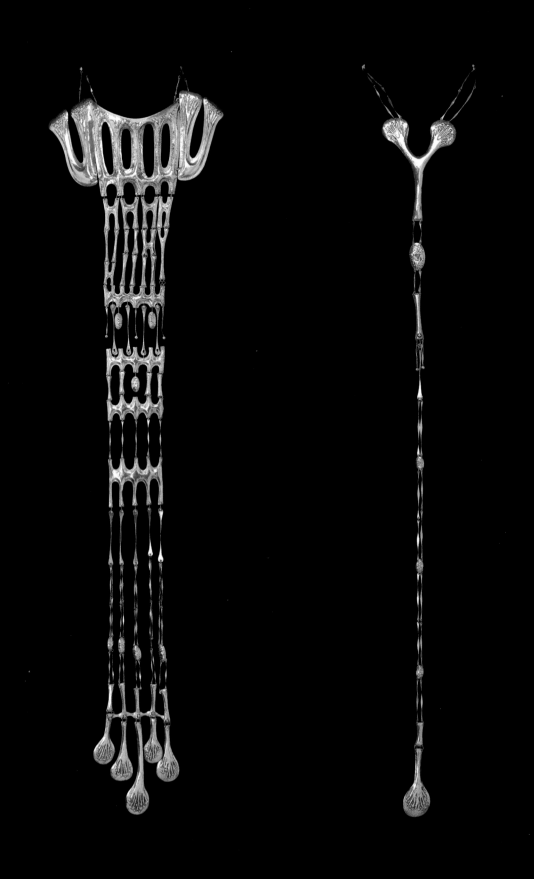

Arline M. Fisch (United States, 1931–)
Body Ornament, front and back · 1966

Silver
45 x 12 ¹/₄ in. (114.3 x 31.1 cm)
41 x 4 ¹/₂ in. (104.1 x 10.8 cm)
Gift of the Johnson Wax Company,
through the American Craft Council, 1977

Alma Eikerman (United States, 1908–1995)
Bracelet · 1968

Silver
3 ³/₈ x 3 x 1 ¹/₄ in. (8.6 x 7.6 x 3.2 cm)
Gift of the Johnson Wax Company, through the American Craft Council, 1978

Art Smith (United States, 1923–1982)
Neckpiece · 1967

Silver, crystal
4 ³⁄₄ x 4 x 2 ¹⁄₄ in. (12.1 x 10.2 x 5.7 cm)
Gift of Stanley Seidman, through the American Craft Council, 1967

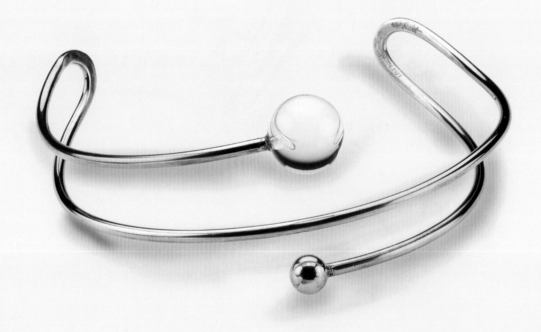

Vivianna Torun Bülow-Hübe (Sweden, 1927–2004, Indonesia)
Necklace and Brooch · c. 1965

Silver, mother of pearl
8 ¹⁄₄ x 5 ¹⁄₂ x ³⁄₈ in. (21 x 14 x 1 cm), necklace
2 ¹⁄₄ x 1 x ¹⁄₄ in. (5.7 x 2.5 x 0.6 cm), brooch
Museum purchase with funds provided by the Collections Committee, 2005

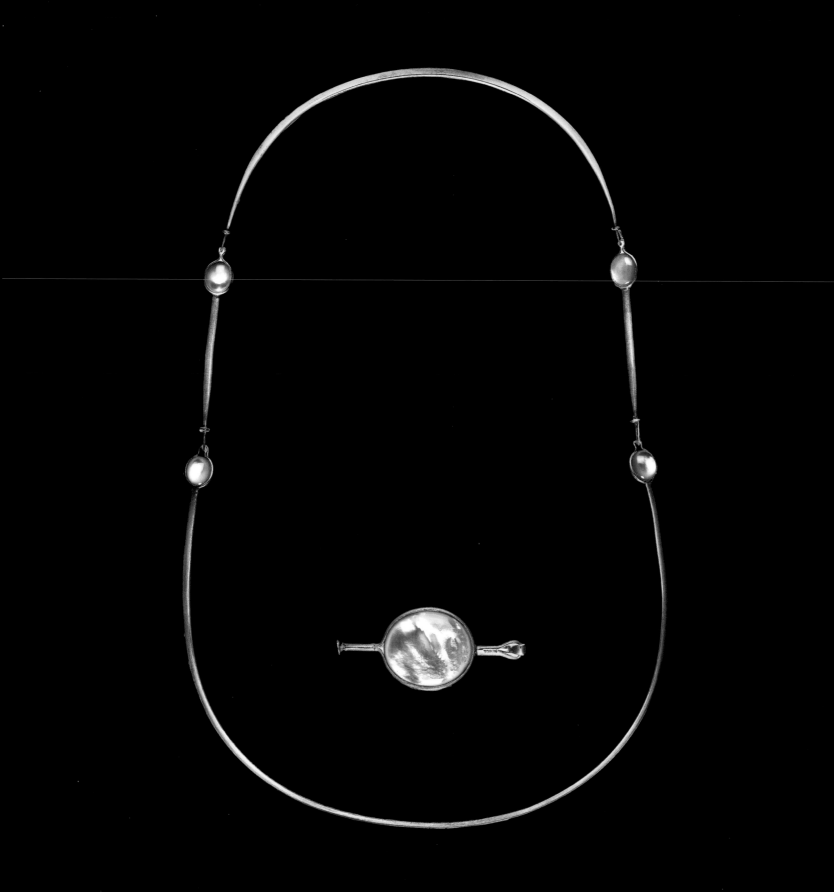

Ken Cory (United States, 1943–1994)
Brooch · 1968

Copper, Plexiglas
2 1/8 x 2 5/8 x 5/8 in. (5.4 x 6.7 x 1.6 cm)
Gift of the Johnson Wax Company, through the American Craft Council, 1977

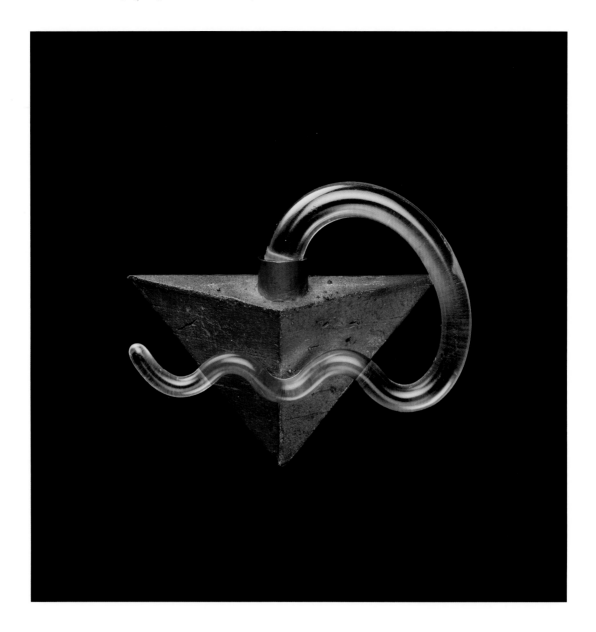

J. Fred Woell (United States, 1934–)
The Good Guys (pendant) · 1966

Walnut, steel, copper, plastic, silver, gold leaf
4 x 1/2 in. (10.2 x 1.3 cm), diameter x depth
Gift of the Johnson Wax Company, through the American Craft Council, 1977

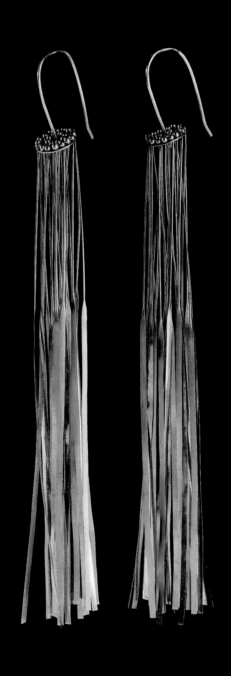

Phillip Fike (United States, 1927–1997)
Earrings · 1968

Gold
3 ⁷/₈ x ³/₈ x ¹/₂ in. (9.8 x 1 x 1.3 cm), each
Gift of the Johnson Wax Company, through the American Craft Council, 1977

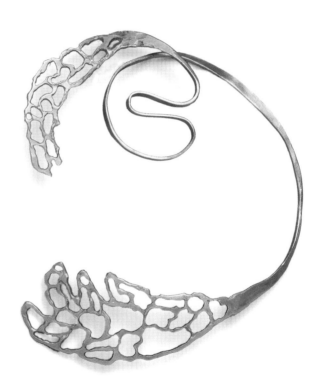

Irena Brynner (Russia, 1917–2003, United States)
Earrings · 1967

Gold
3 ³/₈ x 3 x ¹/₂ in. (8.6 x 7.6 x 1.3 cm), each
Gift of the Johnson Wax Company, through the American Craft Council, 1978

Joe Reyes Apodaca (United States, 1942–)
Ring · **1966**

Gold, rutilated quartz
1 x 1 ¼ x 1 in. (2.5 x 3.2 x 2.5 cm)
Gift of the Johnson Wax Company, through the American Craft Council, 1977

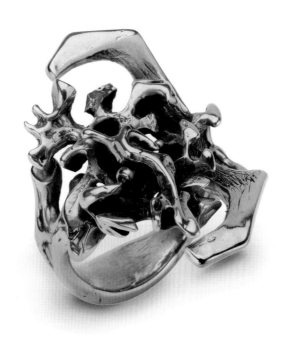

Bob Winston (United States, 1915–2003)
Ring · **1969**

Gold
1 ¹/₈ x 1 x 1 ¹/₄ in. (2.9 x 2.5 x 3.2 cm)
Gift of the Johnson Wax Company, through the American Craft Council, 1977

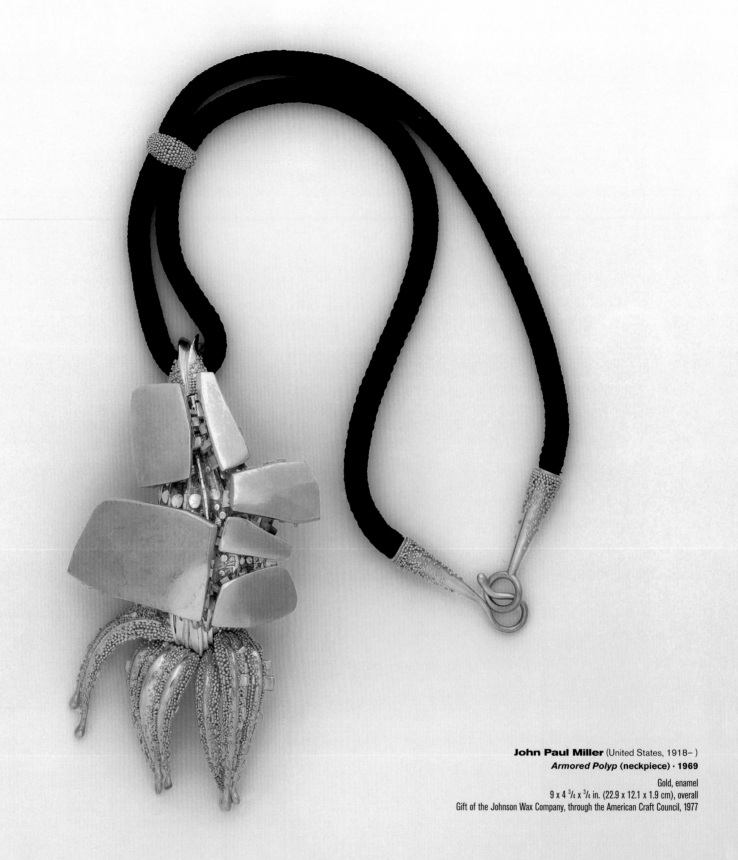

John Paul Miller (United States, 1918–)
Armored Polyp (neckpiece) · **1969**

Gold, enamel
9 x 4 ³/₄ x ³/₄ in. (22.9 x 12.1 x 1.9 cm), overall
Gift of the Johnson Wax Company, through the American Craft Council, 1977

Ruth Radakovich (United States, 1920–1975)
Cocktail Ring · **1969**

Gold, titanium rutile
2 ³/₄ x 1 ⁵/₈ x 1 ⁵/₈ in. (7 x 4.1 x 4.1 cm)
Gift of the Johnson Wax Company, through the American Craft Council, 1977

Ed Wiener (United States, 1918–1991)
Opal Brooch · **c. 1966**

Opal, gold
2 x 3 x ½ in. (5.1 x 7.6 x 1.3 cm)
Gift of Irene Shapiro and Rosalyn Copleman, 2000

Charles Loloma (United States, 1921–1991)
Bracelet, **front and back · 1968**

Silver, turquoise, ivory, ebony, coral
2 ⅝ x 2 x 1 ½ in. (6.7 x 5.1 x 3.8 cm)
Gift of the Johnson Wax Company, through the American Craft Council, 1977

Ramona Solberg (United States, 1921–2005)
Shaman's Necklace · **1968**

Silver, Alaskan ivory, found objects
10 ³/₈ x 5 ³/₈ x ³/₄ in. (26.4 x 13.7 x 1.9 cm)
Gift of the Johnson Wax Company, through the American Craft Council, 1977

Otto Künzli

Susanna Heron

Olaf Skoogfors

70s

William Harper

Robert Lee Morris

Ibram Lassaw

Richard Mawdsley

Mary Ann Scherr

Caroline Broadhead

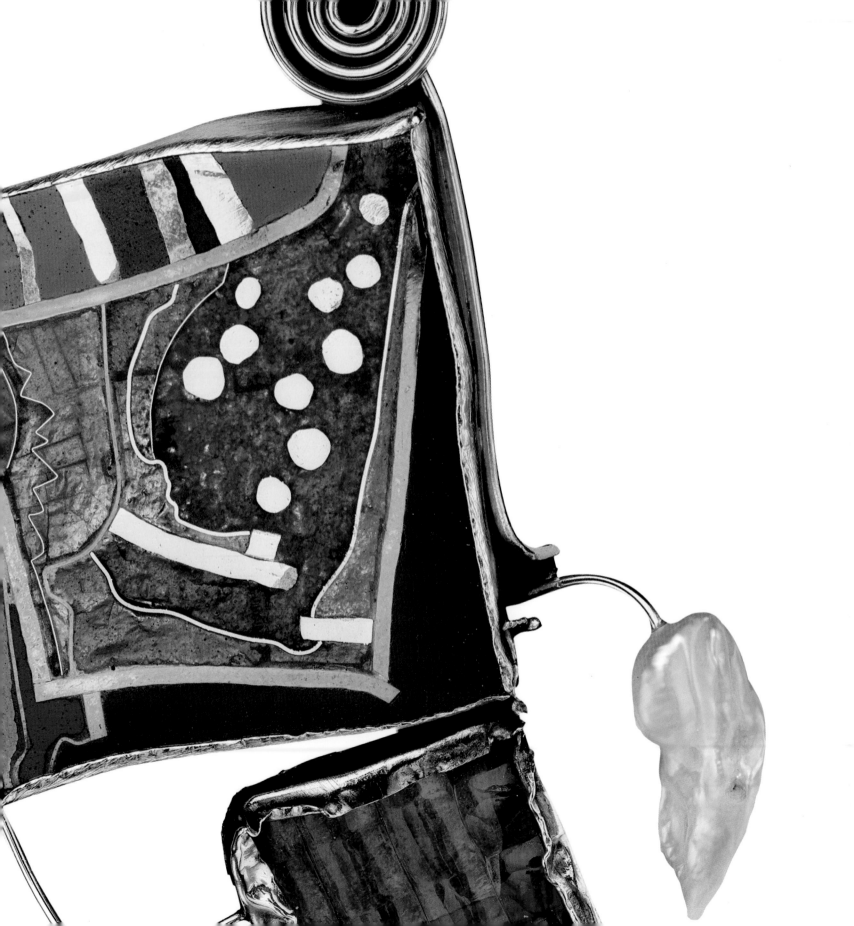

Otto Künzli (Switzerland, 1948–current residence, Germany)
Brooch · **1979**

Silver, gold
1 ³/₄ x 1 ³/₄ x 1 in. (4.4 x 4.4 x 2.5 cm)
Gift of Donna Schneier, 1997

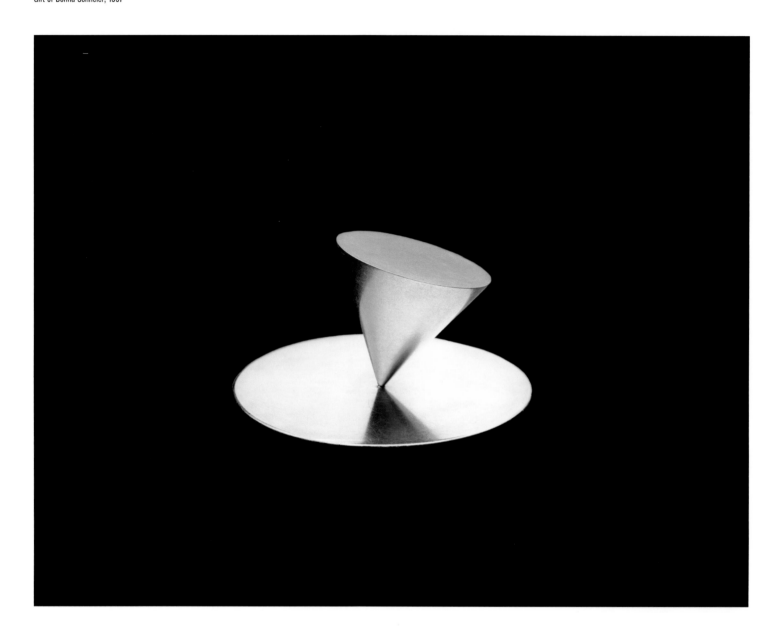

Susanna Heron (England, 1949–)
Jubilee Neckpiece · **1977**

Plexiglas, polyester resin
18 x 18 x ¹/₈ in. (45.7 x 45.7 x 0.3 cm)
Gift of Donna Schneier, 1997

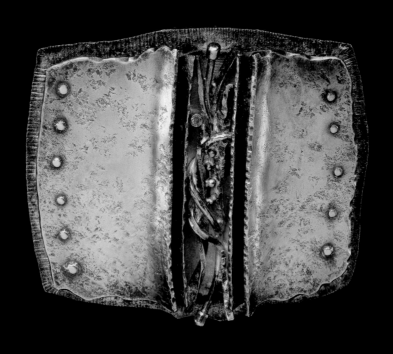

Olaf Skoogfors (Sweden, 1930–1975, United States)
Brooch · 1975
Silver, gold plate
2 1/8 x 2 3/8 x 1/2 in. (5.4 x 6 x 1.3 cm)
Gift of Edna S. Beron, 1990

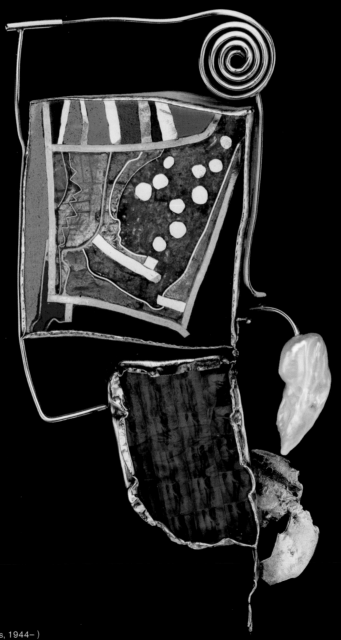

William Harper (United States, 1944–)
Transfigured Mystery **(brooch)** · **1979**

Gold, silver, cloisonné enamel on copper, baroque pearl, bicycle reflector
4 ³/₈ x 2 ³/₈ x ¹/₂ in. (11.1 x 6 x 1.3 cm)
Museum purchase with funds donated by the Barbara Rockefeller Foundation, 1993

Robert Lee Morris (Germany, 1947–current residence, United States)
Verdigris Herringbone Collar · **1978**
Patinated brass
6 x 6 x 1 ¹/₂ in. (15.2 x 15.2 x 3.8 cm)
Gift of the artist, 2008

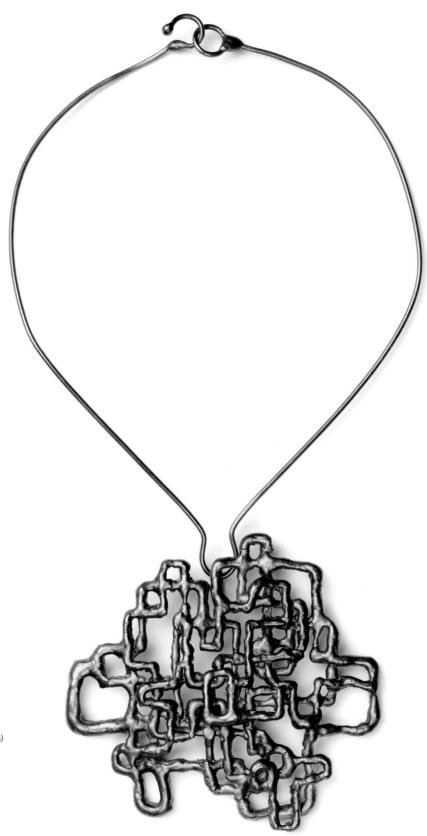

Ibram Lassaw (Egypt, 1913–2003, United States)
Neckpiece · **1972**

Gold-plated bronze
9 x 4 $^1/_2$ x $^1/_2$ in. (22.9 x 11.4 x 1.3 cm), overall
3 x 3 $^1/_2$ x $^1/_2$ in. (7.6 x 8.9 x 1.3 cm), pendant
Gift of Donna Schneier, 1997

Richard Mawdsley (United States, 1945–)
Goneril, Regan, Cordelia (belt buckle) · 1976

Silver, lapis lazuli, coral
3 ³/₈ x 3 ³/₄ x ⁵/₈ in. (8.6 x 9.5 x 1.6 cm)
Purchased by the American Craft Council with funds provided
by the National Endowment for the Arts, 1984

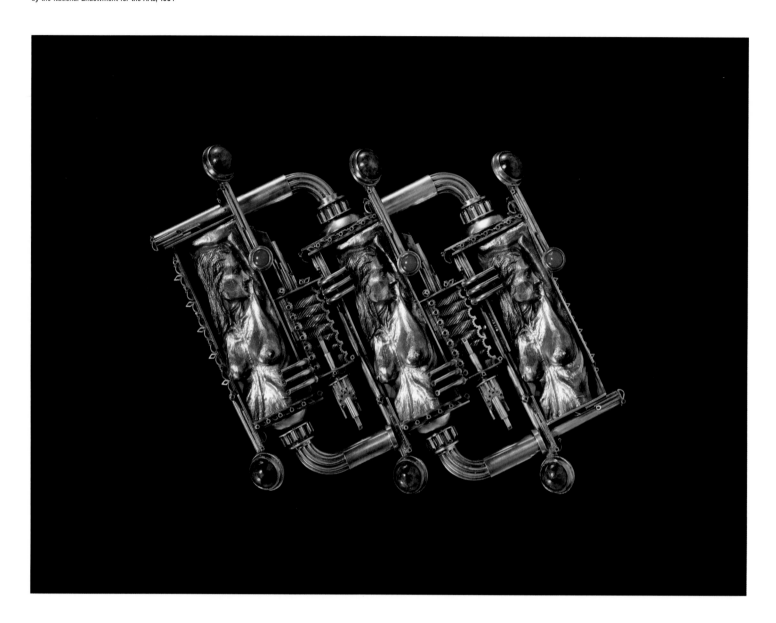

Mary Ann Scherr (United States, 1921–)
Electronic Oxygen Belt Pendant · 1974

Silver, electronics, amber, oxygen mask
12 x 4 x 1 in. (30.5 x 10.2 x 2.5 cm), pendant
Gift of Mary Lee Hu, through the American Craft Council, 1979

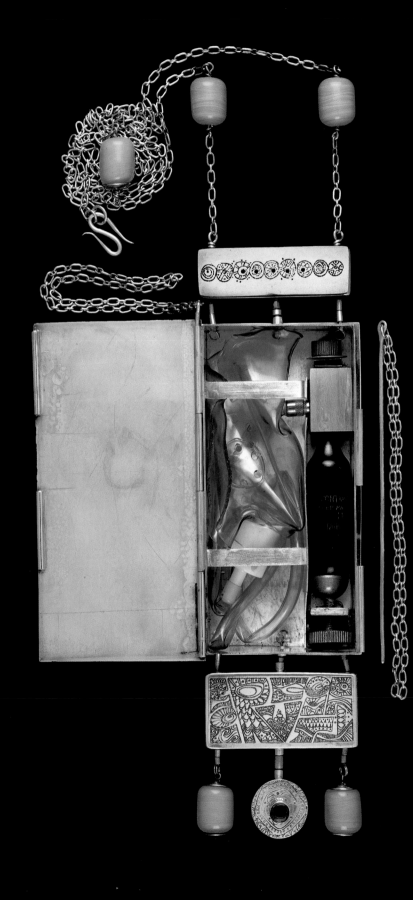

Caroline Broadhead (England, 1950–)
Neckpiece · 1978

Silver, wood, dyed nylon monofilament
8 x 8 x $\frac{3}{8}$ in. (20.3 x 20.3 x 1 cm)
Gift of Donna Schneier, 1997

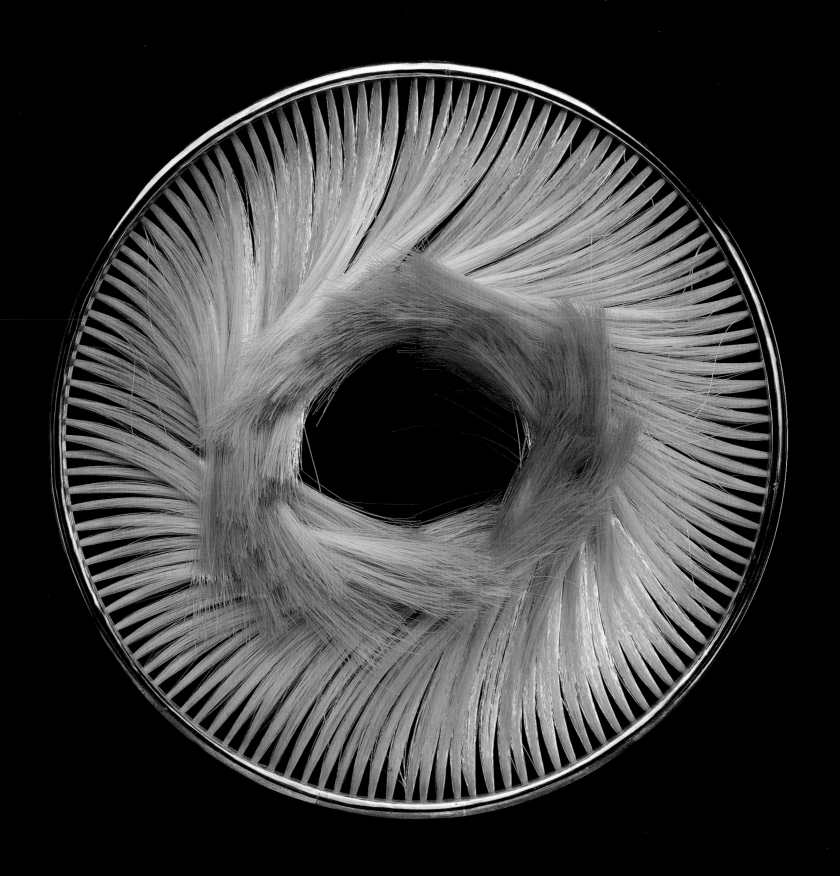

Earl Pardon	David Freda	Lam de Wolf
Jamie Bennett	Pavel Opočenský	Sharon Church
Hermann Jünger	Richard H. Reinhardt	K. Lee Manuel
Robert W. Ebendorf	Rachelle Thiewes	Hiroko Sato Pijanowski
Ivy Ross	Gretchen Raber	Gene Pijanowski
Peter Chang	Myra Mimlitsch-Gray	Marjorie Schick
Otto Künzli	Wilhelm Tasso Mattar	Beatrice Wood
Lisa Gralnick	Julia Manheim	Cara Croninger
David Tisdale	Caroline Broadhead	Esther Knobel
Wendy Ramshaw	Arline M. Fisch	Bruce Metcalf
David Watkins	Verena Sieber-Fuchs	Kiff Slemmons
		Vernon Reed

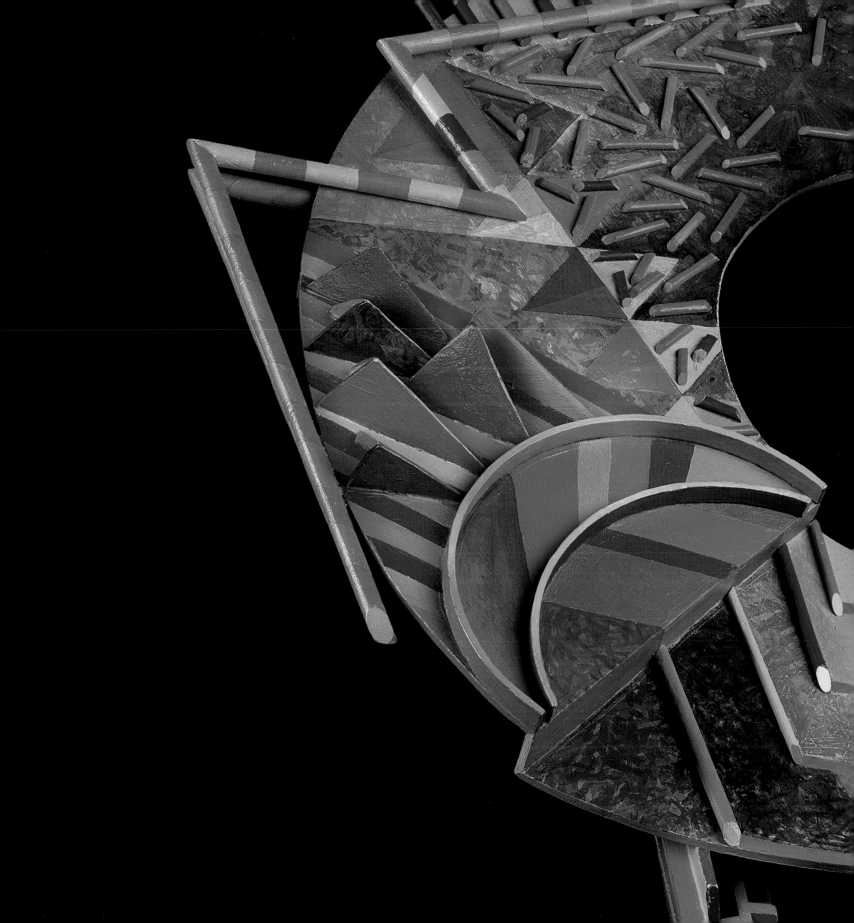

Earl Pardon (United States, 1926–1991)
Necklace · 1983

Gold, black pearl, iridescent shell, opal
1 3/4 x 2 5/8 x 5/16 in. (4.4 x 6.7 x 0.8 cm), pendant
17 1/2 in. (44.5 cm), chain, length
Gift of Herbert Coyne, through the American Craft Council, 1983

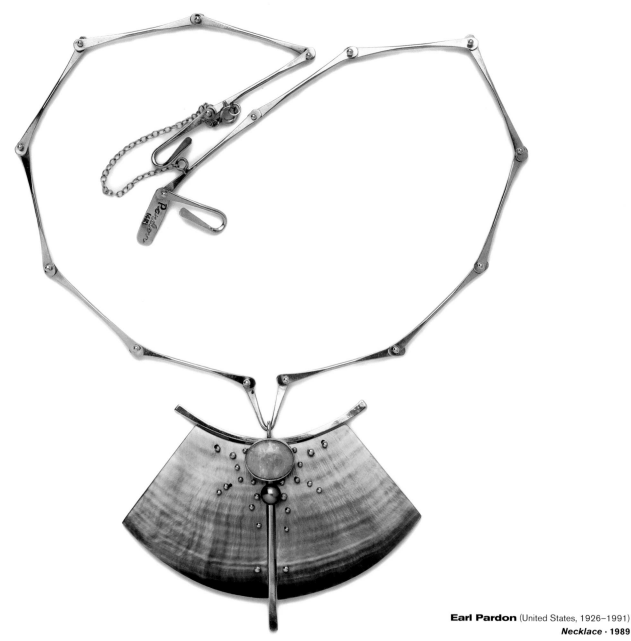

Earl Pardon (United States, 1926–1991)
Necklace · 1989

Cloisonné enamel, gold, silver, gemstones
7 1/2 x 6 x 3/16 in. (19.1 x 15.2 x 0.5 cm)
Gift of Mrs. William Ziff, 1991

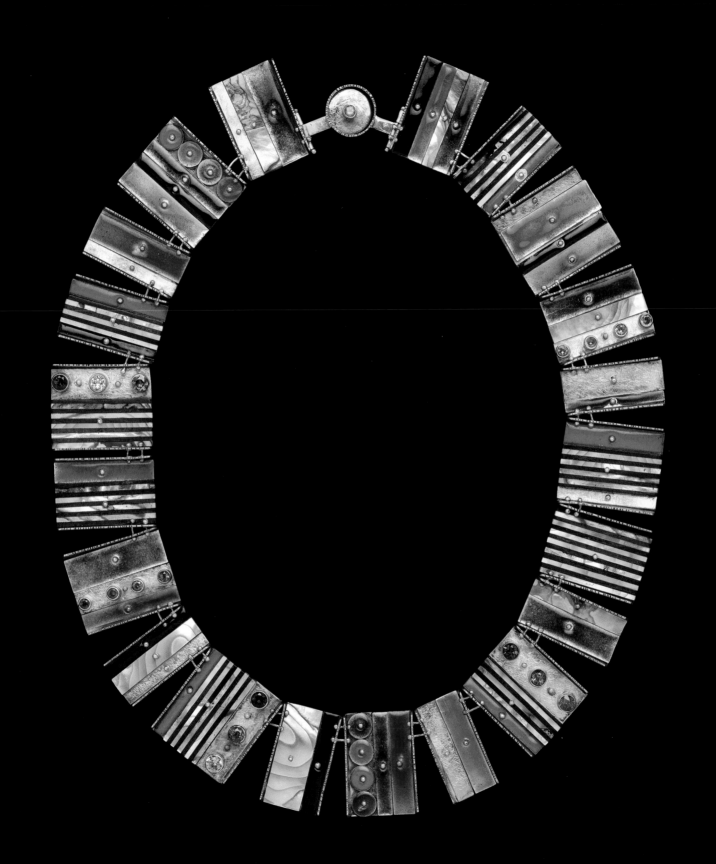

Jamie Bennett (United States, 1948–)
Drawing for *Aiuola Brooch # 19* · 1985–86

Paper, paint, pencil
8 ½ x 6 ¼ in. (21.6 x 15.9 cm)
Gift of the artist, 2005

Jamie Bennett (United States, 1948–)
Aiuola Brooch # 19 · **1988**

Matte enamel, silver, gold, copper, paint
4 ¹/₄ x 3 x ³/₁₆ in. (10.8 x 7.6 x 0.5 cm)
Gift of Romala and Dan Booton, 1993

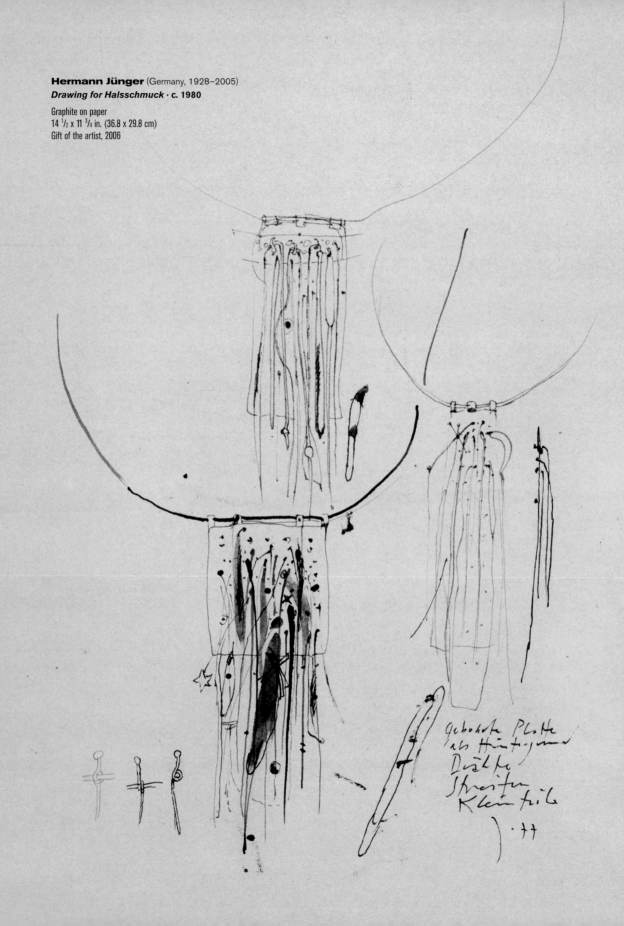

Hermann Jünger (Germany, 1928–2005)
Drawing for Halsschmuck · c. 1980

Graphite on paper
14 1/2 x 11 3/4 in. (36.8 x 29.8 cm)
Gift of the artist, 2006

Hermann Jünger (Germany, 1928–2005)
Halsschmuck (**neckpiece**) · **c. 1980**

Gold, enamel
10 ¹/₂ x 6 ¹/₄ x ¹/₂ in. (26.7 x 15.9 x 1.3 cm), overall
1 ⁹/₁₆ x 2 ³/₈ x ¹¹/₁₆ in. (4 x 6 x 1.8 cm), pendant
Museum purchase with funds provided by the Horace W. Goldsmith Foundation, 2004

Robert W. Ebendorf (United States, 1938–)
Ivy Ross (United States, 1955–)
Necklace · 1986

ColorCore, wooden clothespins, rubber, paint
10 ¹/₂ x 12 ¹/₂ x ¹/₂ in. (26.7 x 31.8 x 1.3 cm)
Gift of Donna Schneier, 1997

Peter Chang (England, 1944–current residence, Scotland)
Bracelet · 1985

Acrylic, polyester, PVC, found objects
6 x 6 x 2 ³/₄ in. (15.2 x 15.2 x 7 cm)
Gift of Jane Korman, 2006

Robert W. Ebendorf (United States, 1938–)
Neckpiece · **1985**
Chinese paper, gold foil, hammered end caps, ebony beads, rubber
12 x 12 x 2 in. (30.5 x 30.5 x 5.1 cm)
Gift of Donna Schneier, 1997

Robert W. Ebendorf (United States, 1938–)
Collar · 1988

Chinese newspaper, wood, paint
12 x 13 x 2 in. (30.5 x 33 x 5.1 cm)
Gift of Donna Schneier, 1995

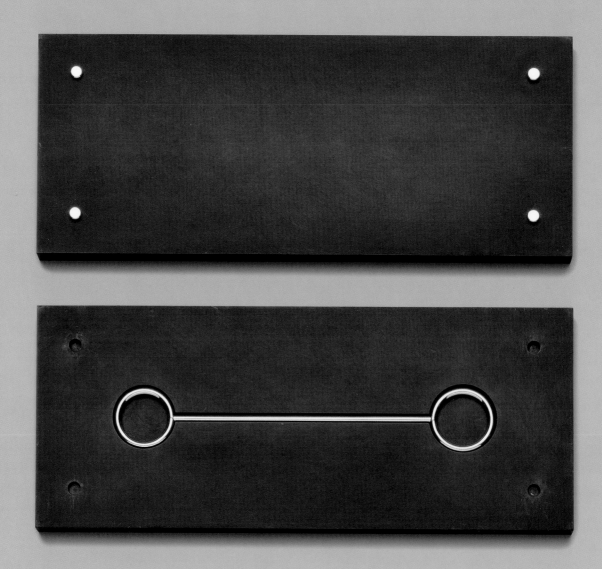

Otto Künzli (Switzerland, 1948–current residence, Germany)
Ring for Two · 1980

Steel, silver, acrylic box
$^3/_4$ x 4 $^3/_4$ x $^1/_8$ in. (1.9 x 12.1 x 0.3 cm), rings
$^3/_4$ x 6 $^5/_8$ x 2 $^3/_4$ in. (1.9 x 16.8 x 7 cm), case, closed
Gift of Donna Schneier, 1997

Otto Künzli (Switzerland, 1948–current residence, Germany)
Gold Makes You Blind · 1980

Rubber, gold
3 $\frac{1}{4}$ x 3 $\frac{1}{8}$ x $\frac{1}{2}$ in. (8.3 x 7.9 x 1.3 cm)
Gift of Donna Schneier, 1997

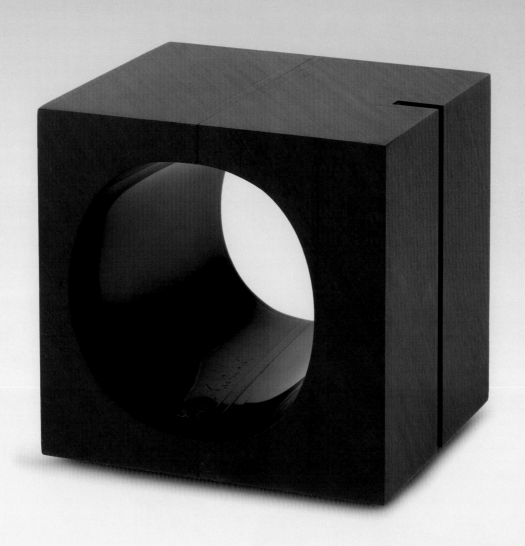

Lisa Gralnick (United States, 1956–)
Bracelet (Cube), **closed · 1988**

Acrylic, gold
3 ⁵/₁₆ x 3 ⁵/₁₆ x 3 ⁵/₁₆ in. (8.4 x 8.4 x 8.4 cm)
Gift of the artist in memory of Joke van Ommen, 1990

Lisa Gralnick (United States, 1956–)
*Bracelet (**Cube**), open · 1988*

Acrylic, gold
3 ⁵/₁₆ x 3 ⁵/₁₆ x 3 ⁵/₁₆ in. (8.4 x 8.4 x 8.4 cm)
Gift of the artist in memory of Joke van Ommen, 1990

David Tisdale (United States, 1956–)
Disk Bracelet · 1982

Anodized aluminum, brass
4 $^1/_2$ x 4 $^1/_2$ x $^3/_4$ in. (11.4 x 11.4 x 1.9 cm)
Gift of the artist, 1995

Wendy Ramshaw (England, 1939–)
Orbit Necklace & Earrings · 1988–89

Nickel alloy, black resin
11 $^1/_4$ x 10 $^3/_8$ x 1 $^7/_8$ in. (28.6 x 26.4 x 4.8 cm), necklace
1 $^1/_8$ x 1 $^1/_8$ x $^1/_4$ in. (2.9 x 2.9 x 0.6 cm), earrings
Gift of Donna Schneier, 1997

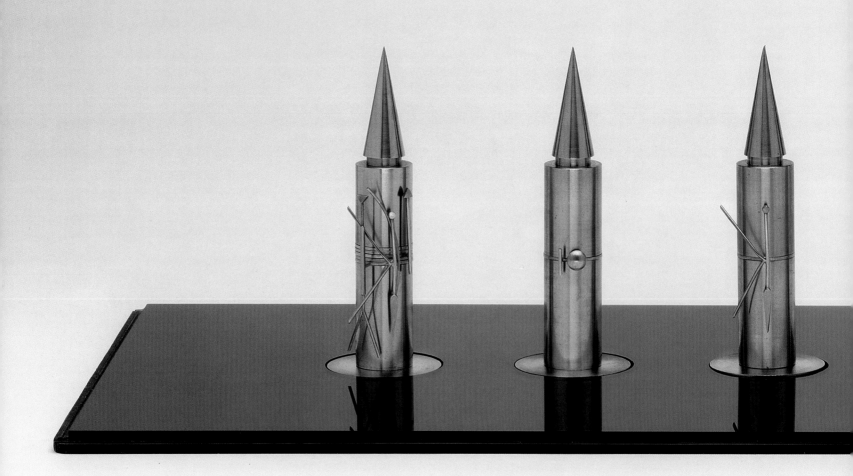

Wendy Ramshaw (England, 1939–)
Set of Six Ring Stands & Rings · 1981

Yellow and white gold, nickel alloy, acrylic
1 x ¾ x 1 ½ in. (2.5 x 1.9 x 3.8 cm), each ring, approximate
4 x ¾ in. (10.2 x 1.9 cm), each stand, height x diameter
Gift of Donna Schneier, 1997

David Watkins (England, 1940–)
Voyager (neckpiece) · 1984–85

Neoprene-coated wood, paint
13 1/2 x 13 1/2 x 5/16 in. (34.3 x 34.3 x 0.8 cm)
Gift of Donna Schneier, 1997

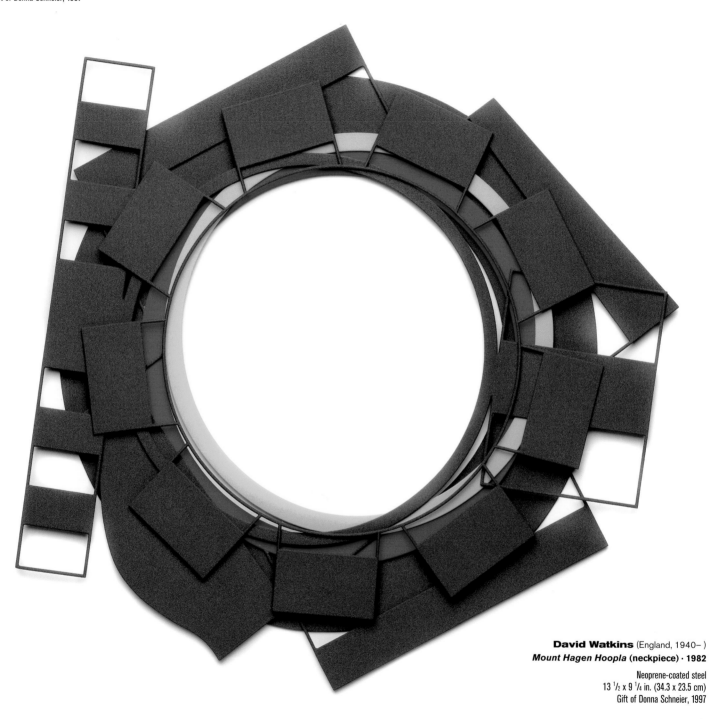

David Watkins (England, 1940–)
Mount Hagen Hoopla (neckpiece) · 1982

Neoprene-coated steel
13 1/2 x 9 1/4 in. (34.3 x 23.5 cm)
Gift of Donna Schneier, 1997

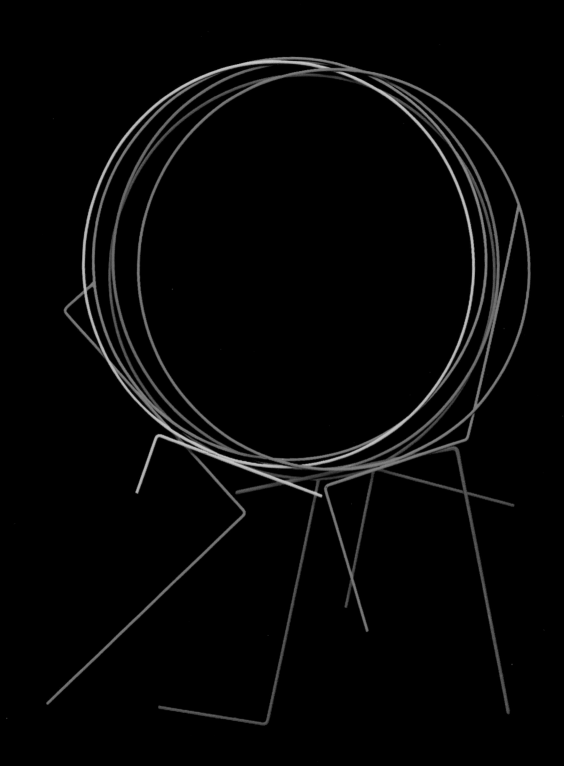

Wendy Ramshaw (England, 1939–)
Wedgwood Pin with Cone-shaped Bead · 1982

Porcelain, gold, pink jasper, gray jasper
1 ³/₄ x 7 ³/₄ x ⁷/₈ in. (4.4 x 19.7 x 2.2 cm)
Gift of Donna Schneier, 1997

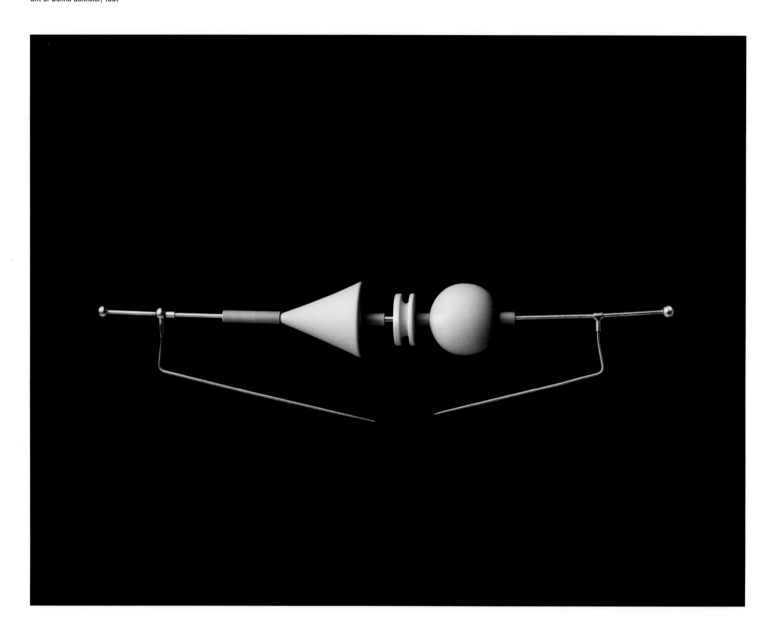

Wendy Ramshaw (England, 1939–)
Wedgwood Necklace · 1982
Ceramic, brass, wire, pink jasper, white jasper
9 ¹/₂ x 11 ¹/₂ x 2 ¹/₂ in. (24.1 x 29.2 x 6.4 cm)
Gift of Donna Schneier, 1997

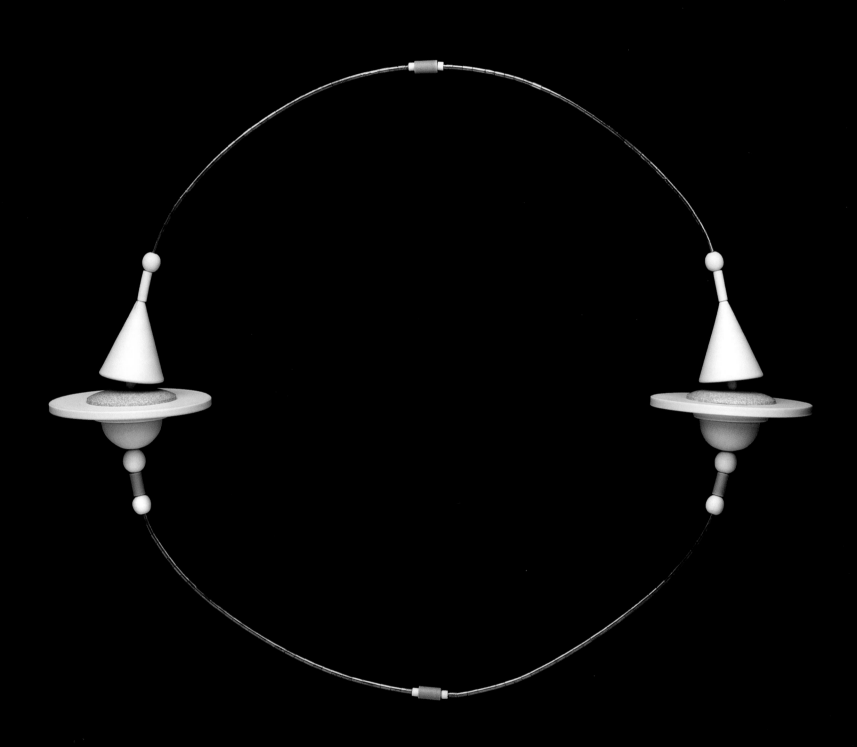

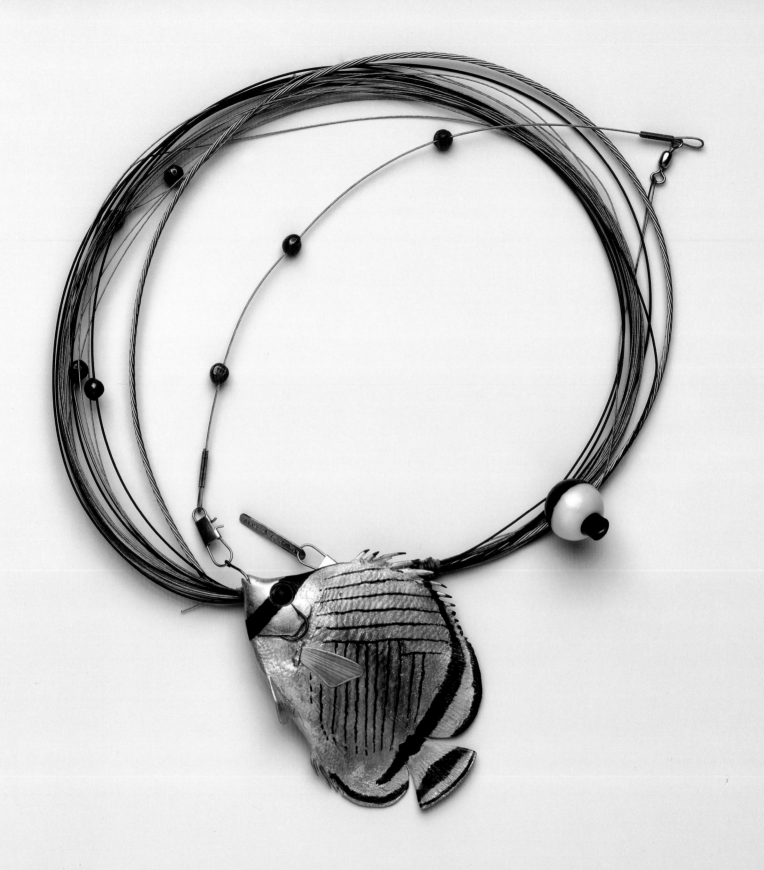

David Freda (United States, 1953–)
Vagabond Butterfly Fish (neckpiece) · **1985**

Enamel, silver, found objects
8 ¹/₂ x 6 x 1 in. (21.6 x 15.2 x 2.5 cm), overall
3 x 2 ¹/₄ x 1 in. (7.6 x 5.7 x 2.5 cm), fish pendant
Gift of Donna Schneier, 1997

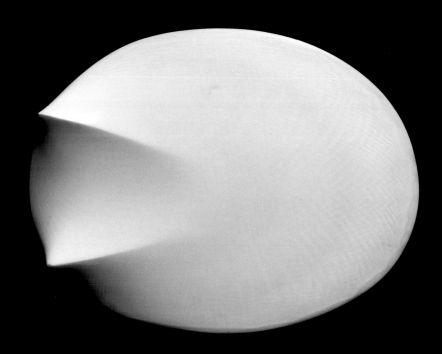

Pavel Opočenský (Czechoslovakia, 1954–
current residence, Czech Republic)
Brooch · **1986**

Ivory
3 ¹/₂ x 2 ⁹/₁₆ x ¹/₂ in. (8.9 x 6.5 x 1.3 cm)
Gift of Donna Schneier, 1997

Richard H. Reinhardt (United States, 1921–1998)
Articulated Necklace · **1988**

Silver
14 ¹/₄ x 7 ¹/₂ x 1 in. (36.2 x 19.1 x 2.5 cm)
Gift of Jane and Leonard Korman, 2008

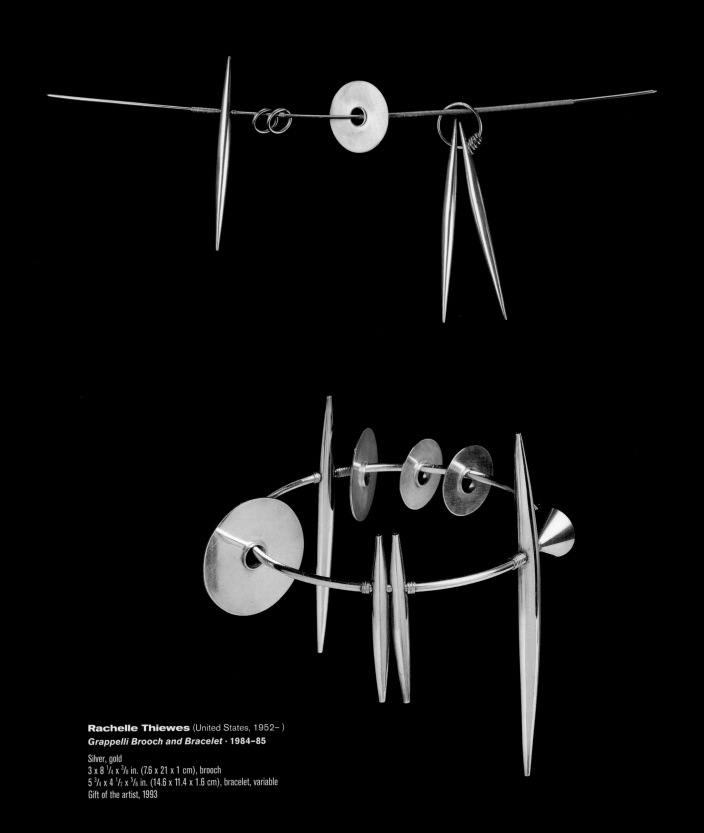

Rachelle Thiewes (United States, 1952–)
Grappelli Brooch and Bracelet · 1984–85

Silver, gold
3 x 8 ¹/₄ x ³/₈ in. (7.6 x 21 x 1 cm), brooch
5 ³/₄ x 4 ¹/₂ x ⁵/₈ in. (14.6 x 11.4 x 1.6 cm), bracelet, variable
Gift of the artist, 1993

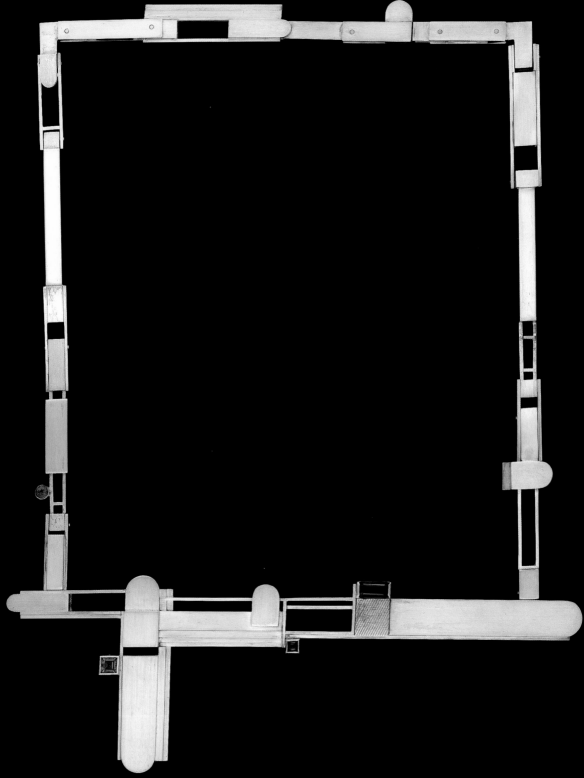

Gretchen Raber (United States, 1943–)
Bi-Radial Necklace · 1988

Silver, gold, emerald, tourmaline
9 x 6 ³/₈ x ³/₈ in. (22.9 x 16.2 x 1 cm)
Gift of the artist's children,
Christianna Irene and Kurt Christian Raber, 1993

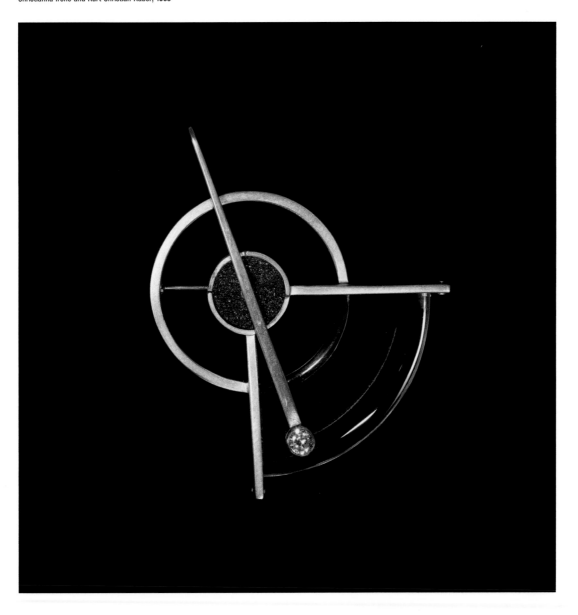

Myra Mimlitsch-Gray (United States, 1962–)
Timepiece (brooch) · 1988

Silver, stainless steel, glass, cubic zirconium, carborundum
2 ¹/₂ x 2 x ¹/₄ in. (6.4 x 5.1 x 0.6 cm)
Promised gift of Susan Grant Lewin, 2008

109

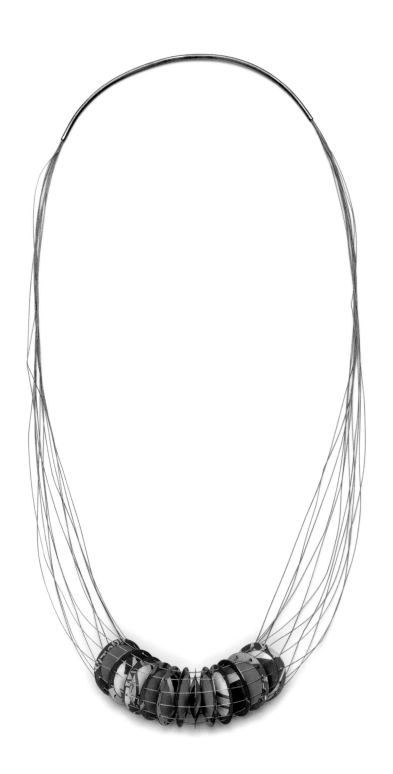

Wilhelm Tasso Mattar (Germany, 1946–current residence, Mallorca)
Coca-Cola Nivea Necklace · **1982**

Steel string, tin
9 $^1/_2$ x 7 x $^1/_2$ in. (24.1 x 17.8 x 1.3 cm)
Gift of Donna Schneier, 1997

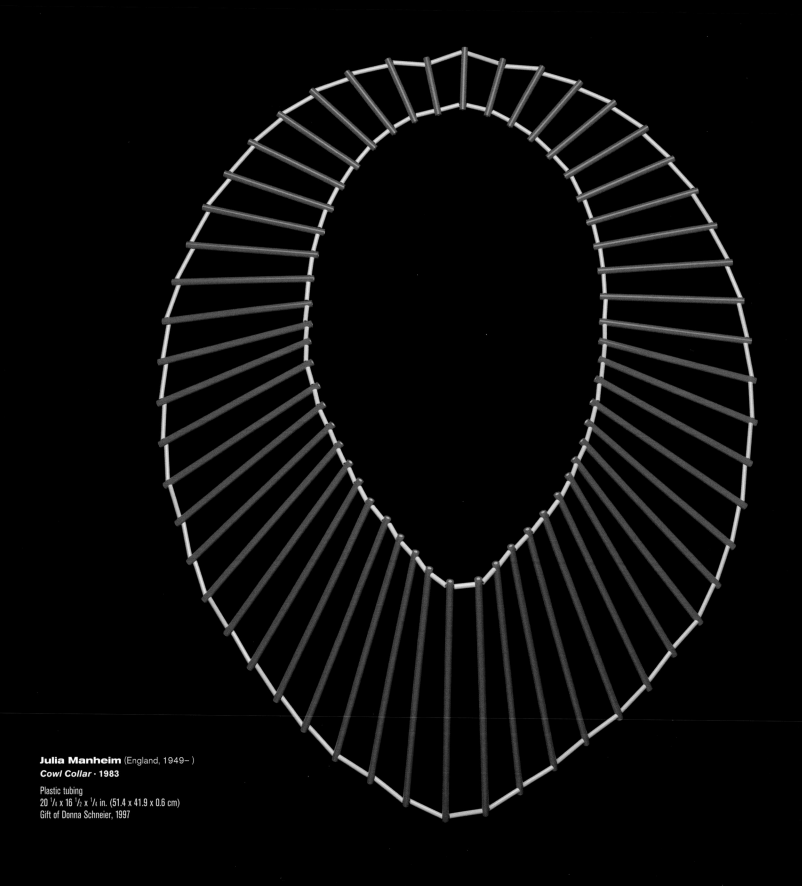

Julia Manheim (England, 1949–)
Cowl Collar · 1983

Plastic tubing
20 $\frac{1}{4}$ x 16 $\frac{1}{2}$ x $\frac{1}{4}$ in. (51.4 x 41.9 x 0.6 cm)
Gift of Donna Schneier, 1997

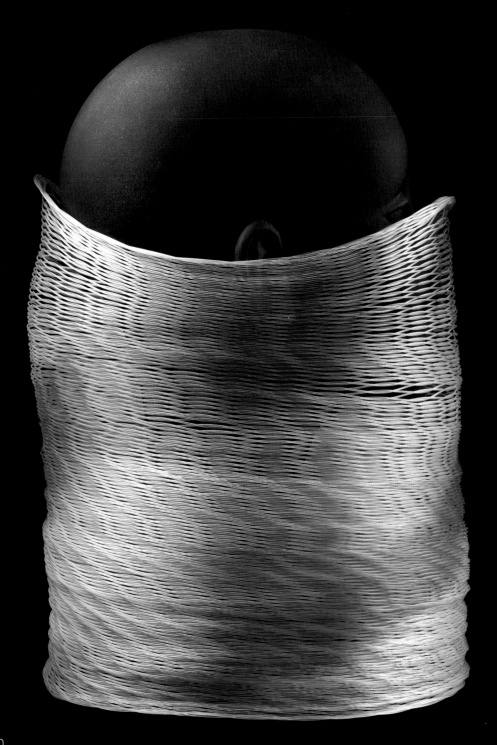

Caroline Broadhead (England, 1950–)
Veil (collar) · 1983

Monofilament, paint
10 ¹/₂ in. (26.7 cm), diameter
31 in. (78.7 cm), length, expanded
Gift of Donna Schneier, 1997

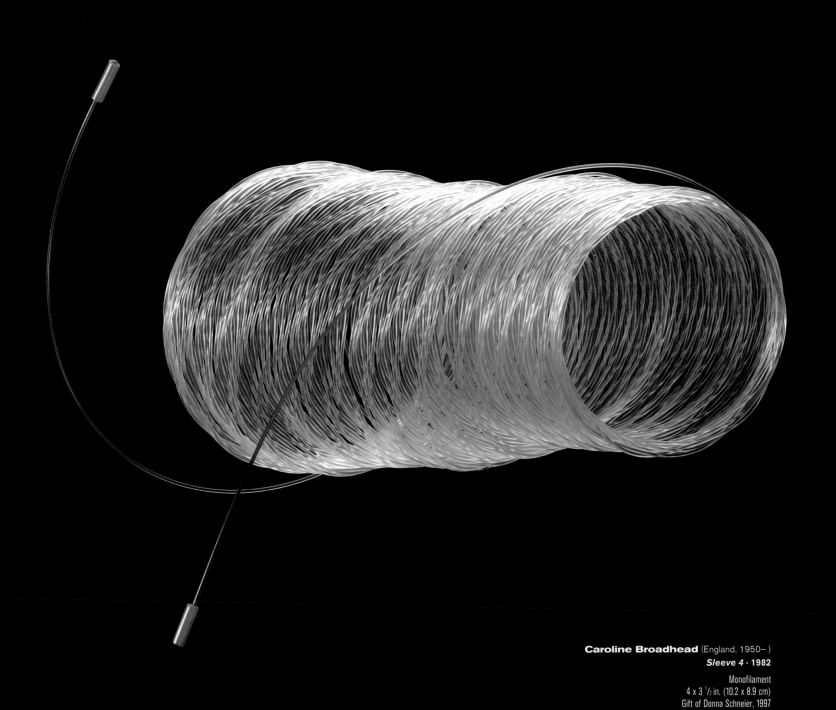

Caroline Broadhead (England, 1950–)
Sleeve 4 · **1982**
Monofilament
4 x 3 ¹/₂ in. (10.2 x 8.9 cm)
Gift of Donna Schneier, 1997

Arline M. Fisch (United States, 1931–)
Cuff MKB67 · 1985
Coated copper, silver
26 x 5 ¾ in. (66 x 14.6 cm), expanded length x diameter
Gift of Donna Schneier, 1997

Arline M. Fisch (United States, 1931–)
Collar MKC38 · 1984

Coated copper, silver
10 x 11 x 2 ¼ in. (25.4 x 27.9 x 5.7 cm)
Gift of the artist, 1991
(detail, left)

Verena Sieber-Fuchs (Switzerland, 1943–)
Firecracker Necklace · **1986**

Firecrackers, firecracker pins, paper, thread, cordite
29 x 8 x 1 ¹/₂ in. (73.7 x 20.3 x 3.8 cm)
Gift of Donna Schneier, 1997

Verena Sieber-Fuchs (Switzerland, 1943–)
Apart-heid (collar) · 1988

Fruit-wrapping tissue paper, wire
16 x 16 x 5 in. (40.6 x 40.6 x 12.7 cm)
Gift of Donna Schneier, 1997

Lam de Wolf (The Netherlands, 1949–)
Yellow Shoulder and Body Piece · **1983**

Silk, paint
17 x 13 x 2 ¼ in. (43.2 x 33 x 5.7 cm)
Gift of Donna Schneier, 1997

Sharon Church (United States, 1948–)
Beaded Collar · 1986

Jasper beads, glass beads, silver, silk
9 x 8 x 1 in. (22.9 x 20.3 x 2.5 cm)
Gift of Rosanne Raab, 2008

Verena Sieber-Fuchs (Switzerland, 1943–)
Head Jewelry · 1986

Paper, wire
3 $^{1}/_{2}$ x 6 $^{1}/_{2}$ in. (8.9 x 16.5 cm), height x diameter
Gift of Donna Schneier, 1997

K. Lee Manuel (United States, 1936–2003)
Protectors of the Sacred Objects of Sirius (collar) · 1988

Goose feathers, suede, paint
22 x 21 x 2 in. (55.9 x 53.3 x 5.1 cm)
Gift of Paul Wittenborn, 1992

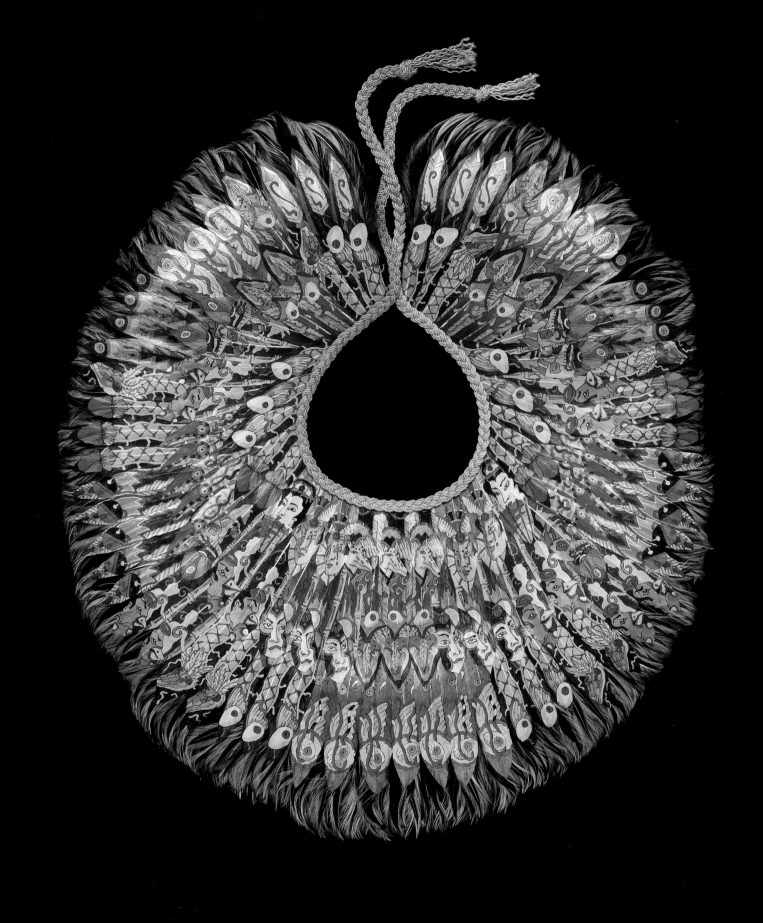

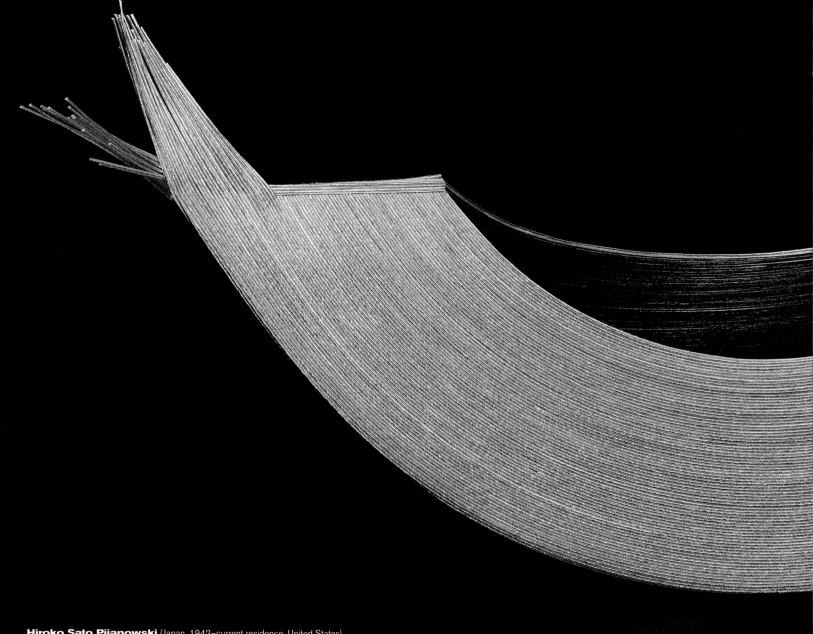

Hiroko Sato Pijanowski (Japan, 1942–current residence, United States)
Gene Pijanowski (United States, 1938–)
Neckpiece Gold No. 1 and *Bracelet Gold No. 1* · **1985**

Paper, string, canvas
9 x 23 x 1 in. (22.9 x 58.4 x 2.5 cm), neckpiece
3 ¹/₄ x 10 x 1 in. (8.3 x 25.4 x 2.5 cm), bracelet
Gift of the artists, 1993

Marjorie Schick (United States, 1941–)
Brooch (with stand) · 1985
Painted wood, brass
14 x 7 x 1 ³⁄₈ in. (35.6 x 17.8 x 3.5 cm)
Gift of Donna Schneier, 1997

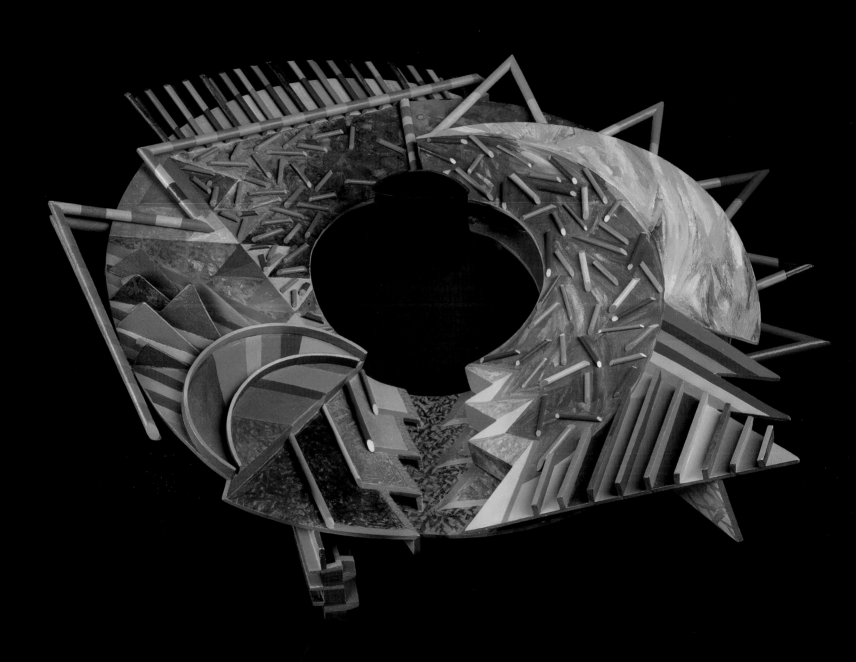

Marjorie Schick (United States, 1941–)
Collar · 1988

Painted wood
25 3/4 x 31 x 6 in. (65.4 x 78.7 x 15.2 cm)
Gift of Dr. James B. M. Schick, Robert M. Schick, and Mrs. Eleanor Krask, 1993

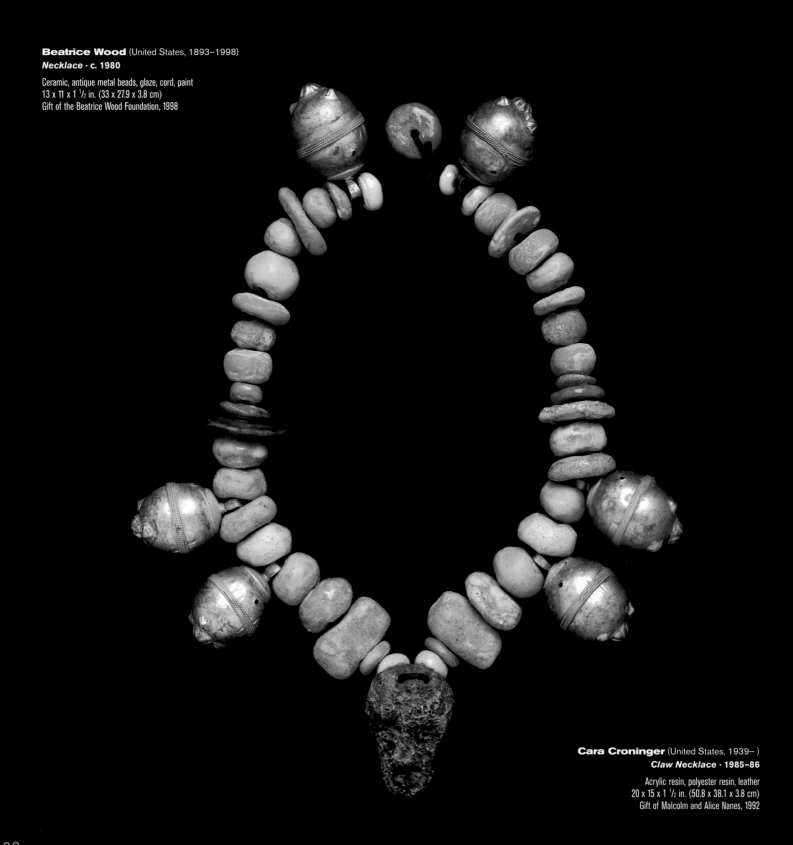

Beatrice Wood (United States, 1893–1998)
Necklace · **c. 1980**

Ceramic, antique metal beads, glaze, cord, paint
13 x 11 x 1 ¹/₂ in. (33 x 27.9 x 3.8 cm)
Gift of the Beatrice Wood Foundation, 1998

Cara Croninger (United States, 1939–)
Claw Necklace · **1985–86**

Acrylic resin, polyester resin, leather
20 x 15 x 1 ¹/₂ in. (50.8 x 38.1 x 3.8 cm)
Gift of Malcolm and Alice Nanes, 1992

128

Esther Knobel (Poland, 1949–current residence, Israel)
#12 Hobeman **(brooch)** · **1985**

Tin, paint
5 ¹/₂ x 3 ¹/₂ x ¹/₄ in. (14 x 8.9 x 0.6 cm)
Gift of Donna Schneier, 1997

Esther Knobel (Poland, 1949–current residence, Israel)
Camouflage Necklace · **1981–82**

Tin, fabric, paint, ribbon, silk cord
13 ³/₄ x 13 ³/₄ x ⁷/₈ in. (34.9 x 34.9 x 2.2 cm)
Gift of Donna Schneier, 1997

Bruce Metcalf (United States, 1949–)
Missing the Prison (brooch) · 1987

Silver, Plexiglas, paint
3 ¹/₄ x 2 ³/₄ x ⁵/₈ in. (8.3 x 7 x 1.6 cm)
Gift of Garth Clark and Mark Del Vecchio, 1992

Kiff Slemmons (United States, 1944–)
Me Too (neckpiece) · 1986

Silver, glass, stone, leather, mirror
10 ¹/₂ x 6 x ³/₈ in. (26.7 x 15.2 x 1 cm)
Promised gift of Mr. and Mrs. Lou Grotta, 2008

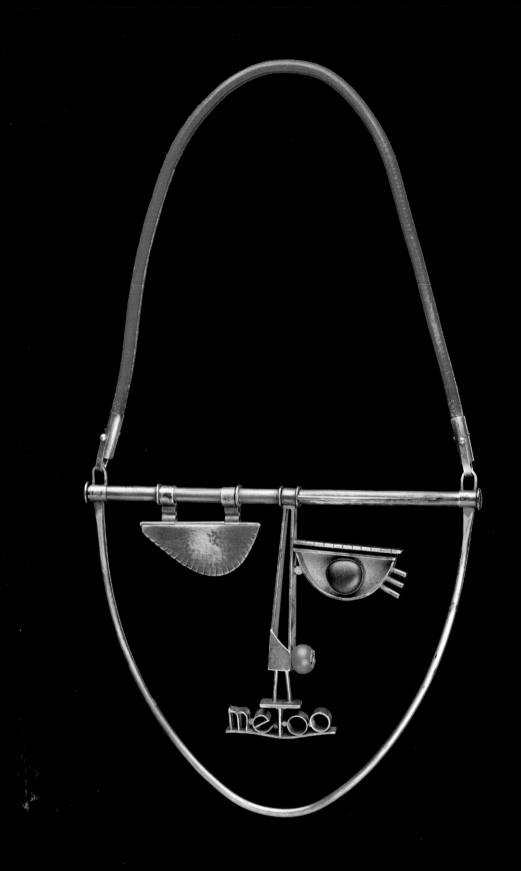

Vernon Reed (United States, 1946–)
Comet Zero (neckpiece) · **1985**

Plexiglas, rubber, metal, battery
9 x 6 x 5 in. (23 x 15.2 x 12.7 cm), removable jewelry
18 x 11 ³/₄ x 2 in. (45.7 x 29.8 x 5.1 cm), display mount
Gift of Donna Schneier, 1997

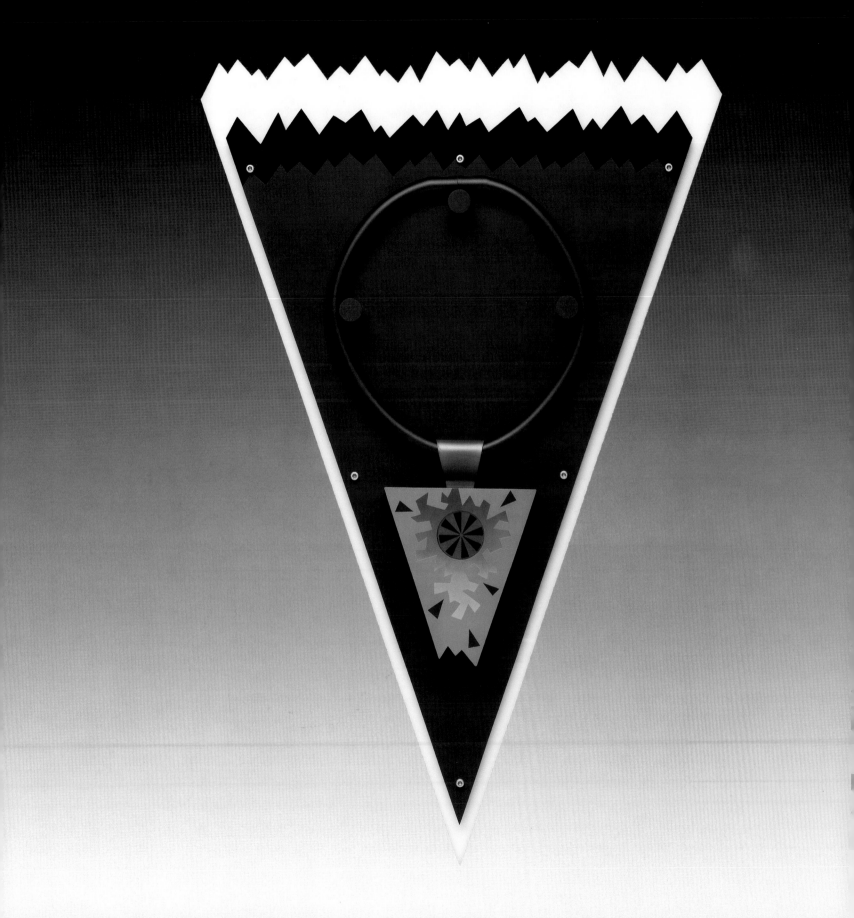

Gijs Bakker

Myra Mimlitsch-Gray

Bruno Martinazzi

Julia Barello

Gerd Rothmann

Marilyn Druin

William Harper

Pierre Cavalan

Wendy Ramshaw

Jeff Wise

Ramón Puig Cuyàs

Daniel Jocz

Thomas Gentille

Eva Eisler

Lisa Spiros

Svenja John

Zack Peabody

Françoise Chavent

Claude Chavent

Julie Anne Mihalisin

Tone Vigeland

Janna Syvänoja

Linda MacNeil

Kim Rawdin

Alberto Zorzi

Richard H. Reinhardt

David Damkoehler

ROY (Rosemary Gialamas)

Richard Mawdsley

Nancy Worden

Pat Flynn

Ted Muehling

Kee-ho Yuen

Enid Kaplan

Jacqueline Lillie

Joyce Scott

Daniella Kerner

Stanley Lechtzin

Keith Lo Bue

Gijs Bakker (The Netherlands, 1942–)
"Borghese" Brooch **from the Holysport series · 1998**

Silver, gold, photograph, Plexiglas
3 $\frac{1}{4}$ x 3 x $\frac{1}{4}$ in. (8.3 x 7.6 x 0.6 cm)
Gift of Helen Williams Drutt English, 2000

Gijs Bakker (The Netherlands, 1942–)
Liberty Brooch · 1997

Executed by Pauline Barendse
Silver, watches
3 ⁷/₈ x 4 ¹/₂ x ³/₈ in. (9.9 x 11.4 x 1 cm)
Promised gift of Mr. and Mrs. Lou Grotta, 2008

Myra Mimlitsch-Gray (United States, 1962–)
Ring II · 1993
Gold
1 x 4 x 2 in. (2.5 x 10.2 x 5.1 cm)
Gift of Donna Schneier, 2000

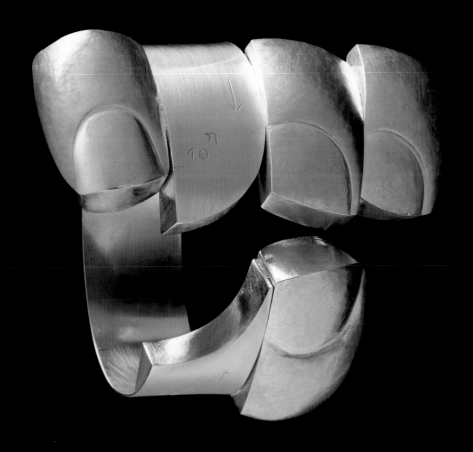

Bruno Martinazzi (Italy, 1923–)
Metamorfosi **(bracelet) · 1992**

Gold
2 ¹/₄ x 3 x 3 ¹/₄ in. (5.7 x 7.6 x 8.3 cm)
Museum purchase with funds provided by Hope Byer, 2006

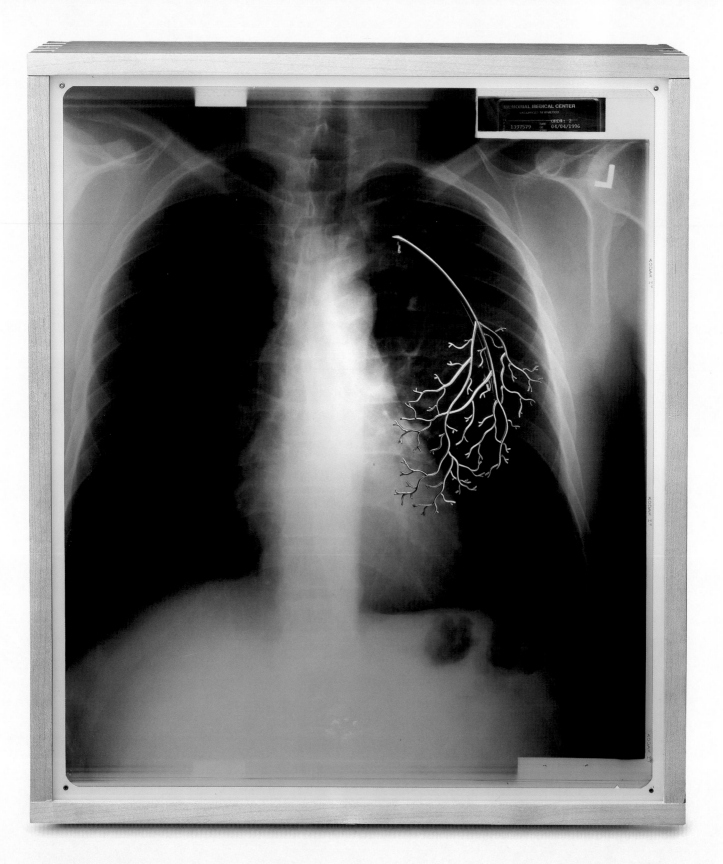

Julia Barello (United States, 1957–)
Vascular Studies II: Lung (brooch) · 1996

Silver, x-ray, maple
18 ⁵⁄₈ x 15 ¹⁄₂ x 7 in. (47.3 x 39.4 x 17.8 cm), light box
5 x 7 x 1 in. (12.7 x 17.8 x 2.5 cm), brooch
Museum purchase with funds provided by Aviva and Jack Robinson, 2006

Gerd Rothmann (Germany, 1941–)
Palm Print (bracelet) · 1997

Sterling silver
4 x 4 x 3 ¹⁄₂ in. (10.2 x 10.2 x 8.9 cm)
Museum purchase with funds provided by the Collections Committee and the Rotasa
Foundation Art Jewelry Grant, 2005

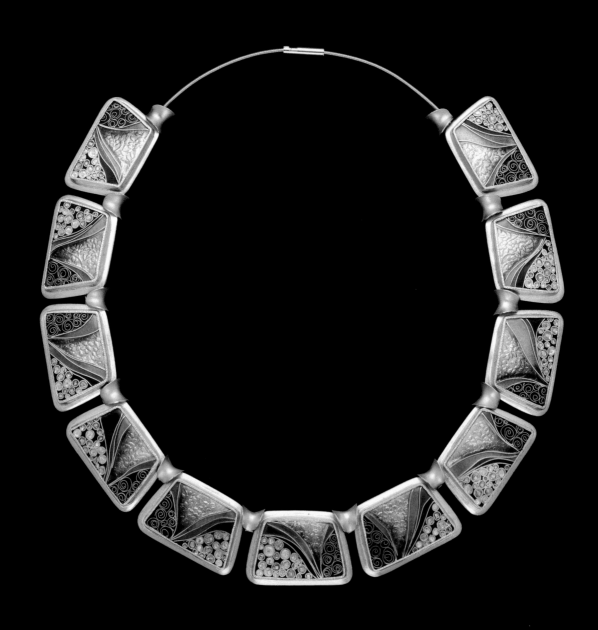

Marilyn Druin (United States, 1941–2001)
Egyptian (necklace) · 1998

Gold, *basse taille* enamel, silver
7 ³/₄ x 7 ¹/₂ x ¹/₂ in. (19.7 x 19.1 x 1.3 cm)
Gift of Mel Druin, Allison Druin, Erica Druin,
and Laura Druin Griffin in memory of Marilyn Druin, 2006

144

William Harper (United States, 1944–)
Shove Causes a Push
(neckpiece for Twyla Tharp dance movement) · 1995

Cloisonné enamel, copper, gold, silver
16 x 15 ½ x 2 ¾ in. (40.6 x 39.4 x 7.0 cm)
Gift of Wendy Evans Joseph, 2001

Pierre Cavalan (France, 1954–current residence, Australia)
Victory (neckpiece) · 1996

Silver, glass, found objects
9 ¹⁄₂ x 9 ¹⁄₂ x ¹⁄₂ in. (24.1 x 24.1 x 1.3cm)
Gift of Helen Williams Drutt English in honor of Barbara Tober, 2007

Wendy Ramshaw (England, 1939–)
Chain of Glass Tears for Weeping Woman
from Picasso's Ladies series · 1998

Glass, blackened steel
18 ⁵⁄₈ x 12 x ¹⁄₄ in. (47.3 x 30.5 x 0.6 cm)
Gift of Barbara Tober, 2005

146

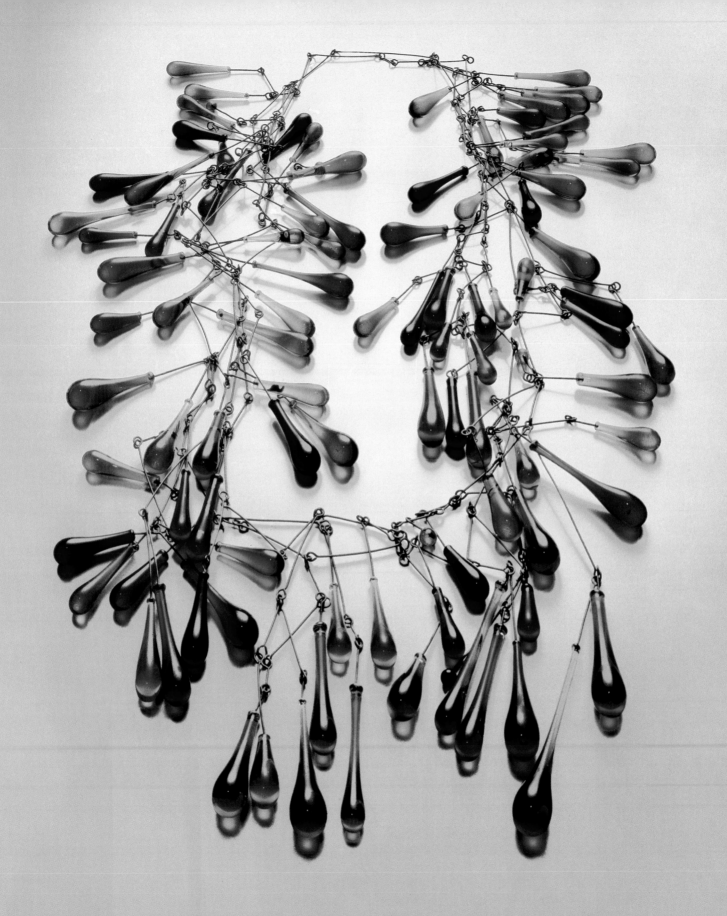

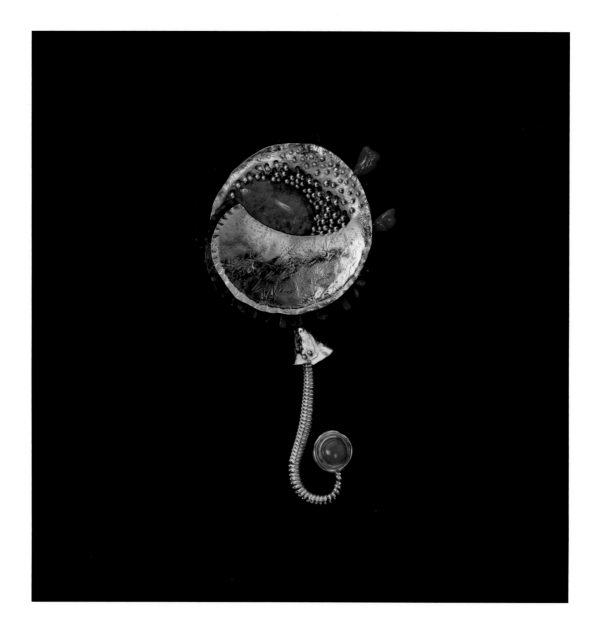

Jeff Wise (United States, 1953–)
Andromeda Rose Up (brooch) · 1996

Gold, lapis lazuli, opal, coral, black jade
4 ⁵/₁₆ x 2 ¹/₂ x ³/₈ in. (11 x 6.4 x 1 cm)
Museum purchase with funds provided by the Horace W. Goldsmith Foundation, 1998

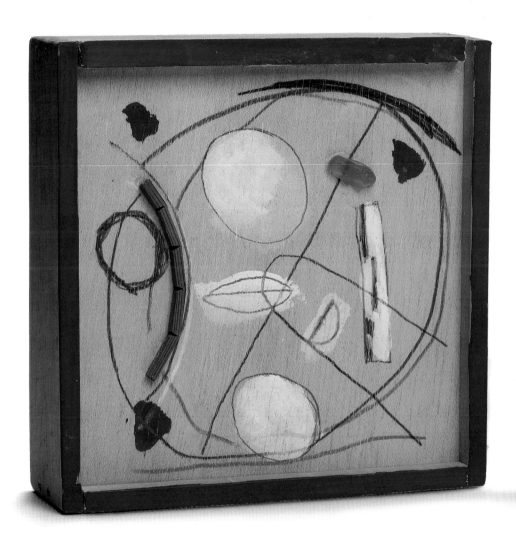
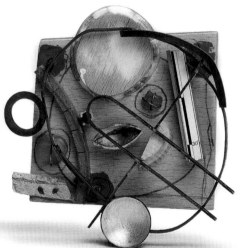

Ramón Puig Cuyàs (Spain, 1953–current residence, United States)
Sempre Cap al Sud (brooch) · 1998

Wood, silver, nickel silver, glass, paper
3 x 3 x ⁵⁄₈ in. (7.6 x 7.6 x 1.6 cm)
6 ¹⁄₈ x 6 ¹⁄₈ x 1 ³⁄₄ in. (15.6 x 15.6 x 4.4 cm), box
Gift of Mimi S. Livingston, 2007

Daniel Jocz (United States, 1943–)
Blue Circle (ring) from the Protos series · 1992

Nickel, polymer clay, pigment
2 x 1 x ¼ in. (5.1 x 2.5 x 0.6 cm)
Gift of Mobilia Gallery and Helen Bock, 1995

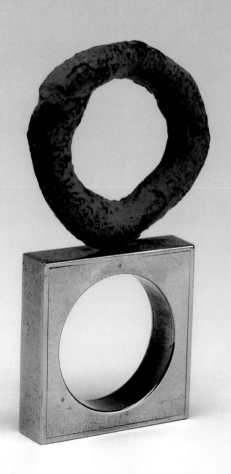

Thomas Gentille (United States, 1936–)
Pin · **1991**

Synthetic resin, pigment
4 ¹/₈ x 4 ¹/₈ x ¹/₄ in. (10.5 x 10.5 x 0.6 cm)
Gift of Helen Williams Drutt English in honor of the artist, 1994

Eva Eisler (Czechoslovakia, 1952–current residence, Czech Republic)
Brooch **from the Tension series · 1990**

Stainless steel, silver
2 ¹/₄ x 3 x ³/₄ in. (5.7 x 7.6 x 1.9 cm)
Gift of the artist, 1995

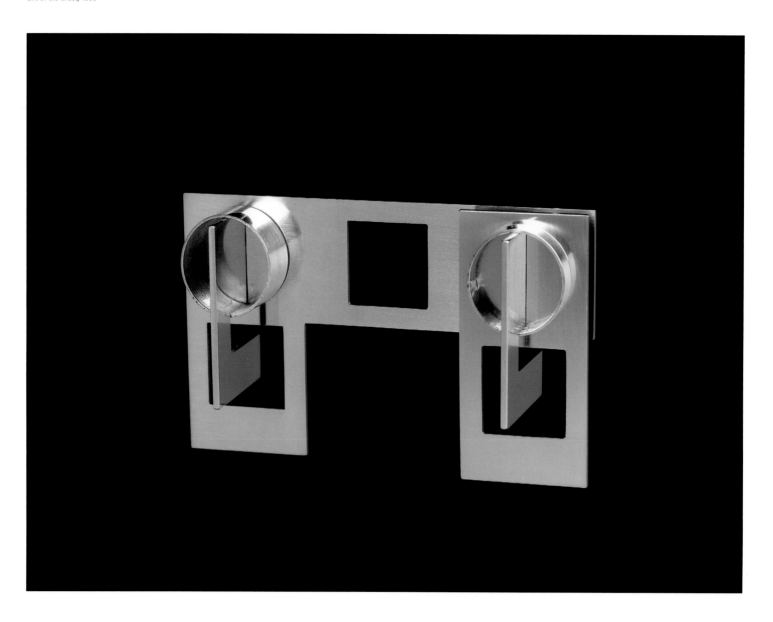

Lisa Spiros (United States, 1959–)
Pendant **· 1992**

Stainless steel
1 ¹/₂ x 4 x ⁵/₈ in. (3.8 x 10.2 x 1.6 cm), pendant
21 ¹/₂ in. (54.6 cm), necklace, length
Gift of the artist, 2008

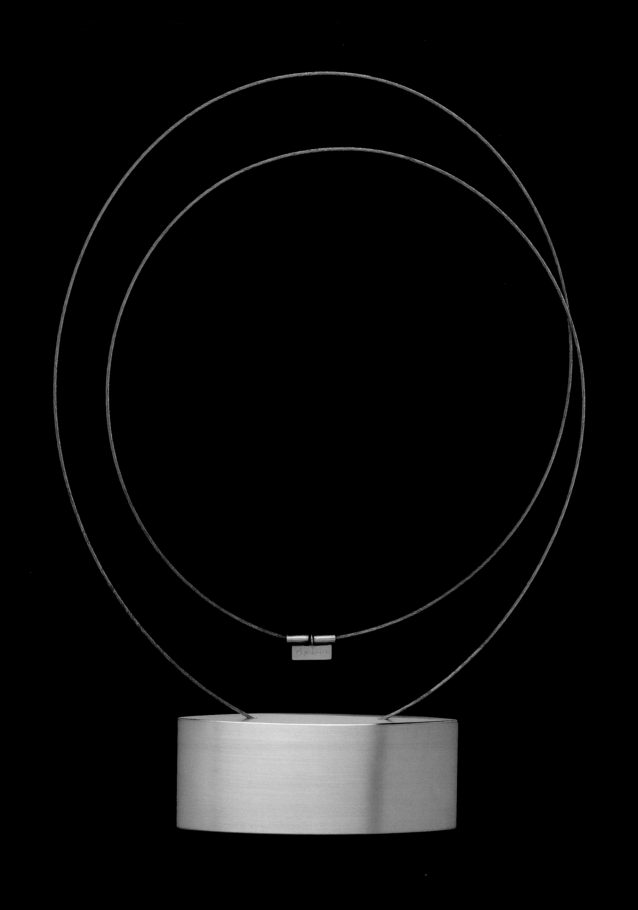

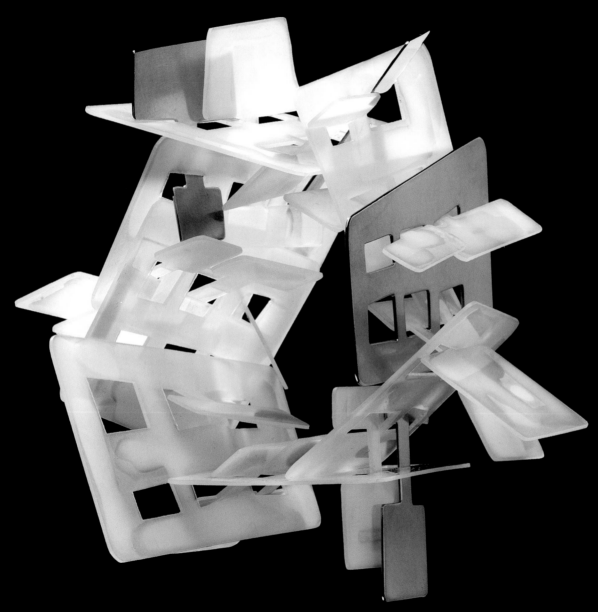

Svenja John (Germany, 1963–)
Bracelet · **1996**

Polycarbonate, steel
4 x 3 ³/₄ x 3 ¹/₂ in. (10.2 x 9.5 x 8.9 cm)
Museum purchase with funds provided by the Horace W. Goldsmith Foundation, 2000

154

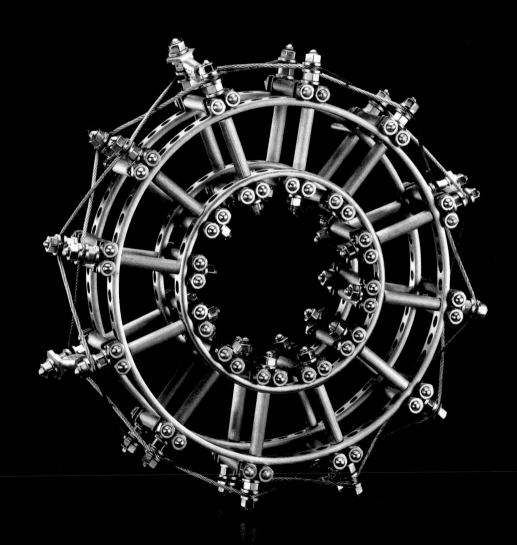

Zack Peabody (United States, 1968–)
Brooch #528 · 1994

Stainless steel, niobium, plated brass, wire, nuts and washers
2 $\frac{7}{8}$ x 2 $\frac{7}{8}$ x 1 $\frac{3}{4}$ in. (7.3 x 7.3 x 4.4 cm)
Gift of the artist, 1995

Françoise Chavent (France, 1947–)
Claude Chavent (France, 1947–)
Tube (brooch) · c. 1999

Silver
2 ¹/₄ x 2 ³/₄ x ¹/₄ in. (5.7 x 7 x 0.6 cm)
Gift of Amy R. Hanan, 2000

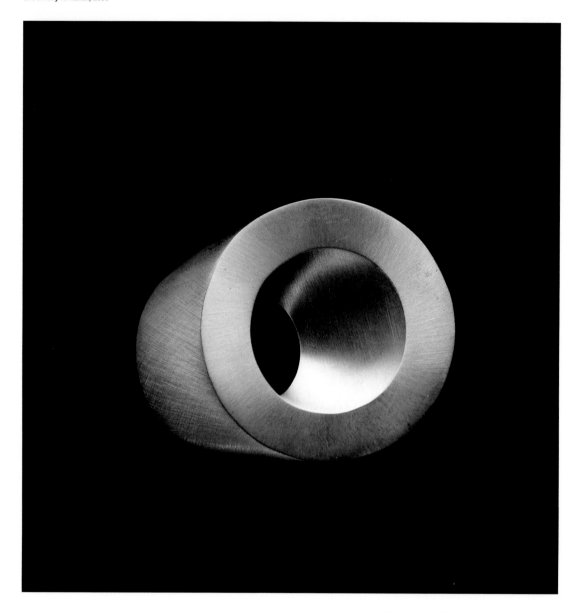

Françoise Chavent (France, 1947–)
Claude Chavent (France, 1947–)
Grand "Cube" (necklace) · c. 1999

Silver, gold
9 x 7 ¹/₂ x 1 ¹/₂ in. (22.9 x 19.1 x 3.8 cm)
Gift of Amy R. Hanan, 2000

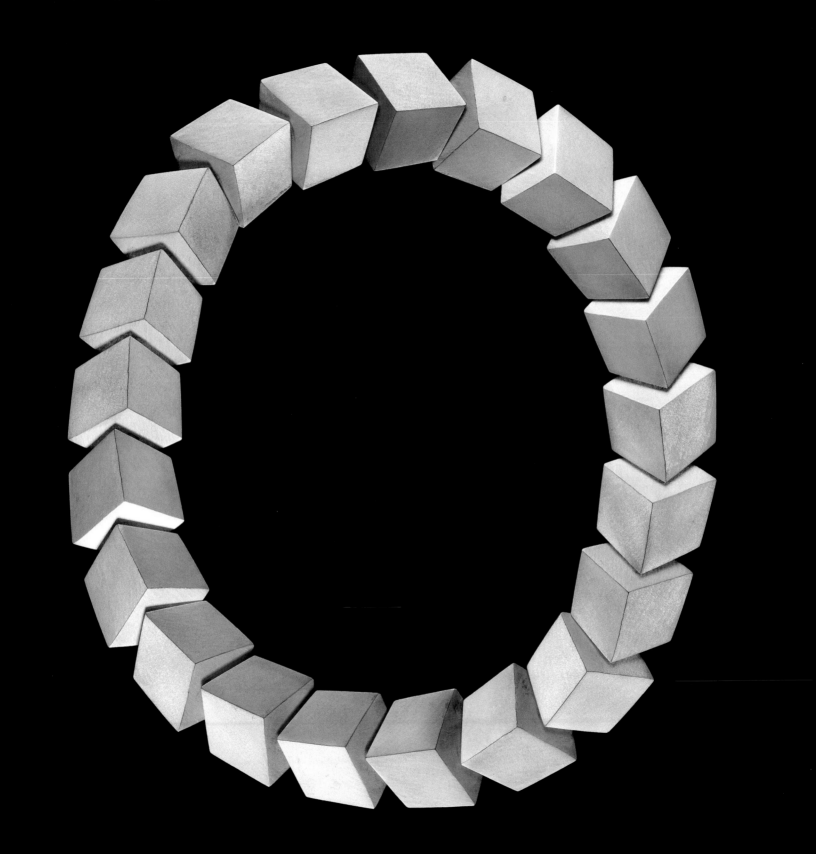

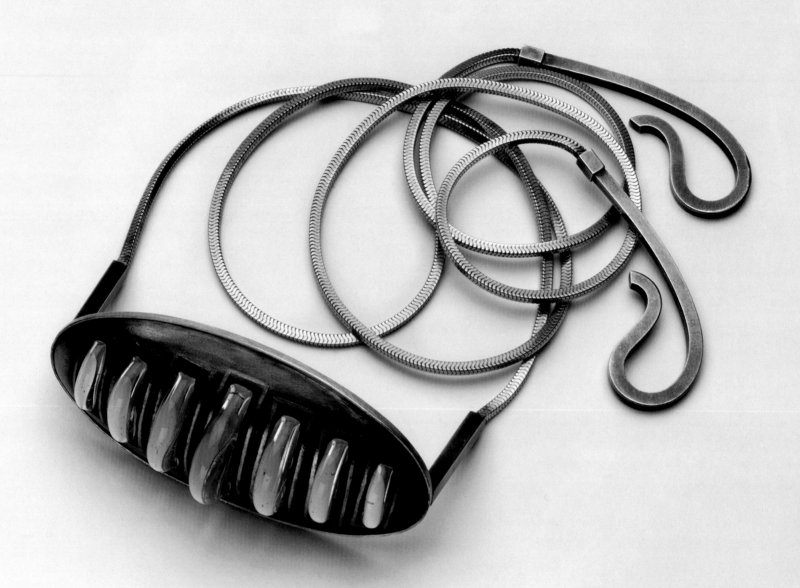

Julie Anne Mihalisin (United States, 1962–)
Window Necklace · 1995

Glass, metal
17 x 5 ¼ x 1 ⅛ in. (43.2 x 13.3 x 2.9 cm)
Museum purchase with funds provided by the Horace W. Goldsmith Foundation, 1999

Tone Vigeland (Norway, 1938–)
Necklace · 1992

Silver
12 $^3/_{16}$ x 5 $^7/_8$ x 1 $^9/_{16}$ in. (31 x 15 x 4 cm)
Museum purchase with funds provided by the Collections Committee, 2000

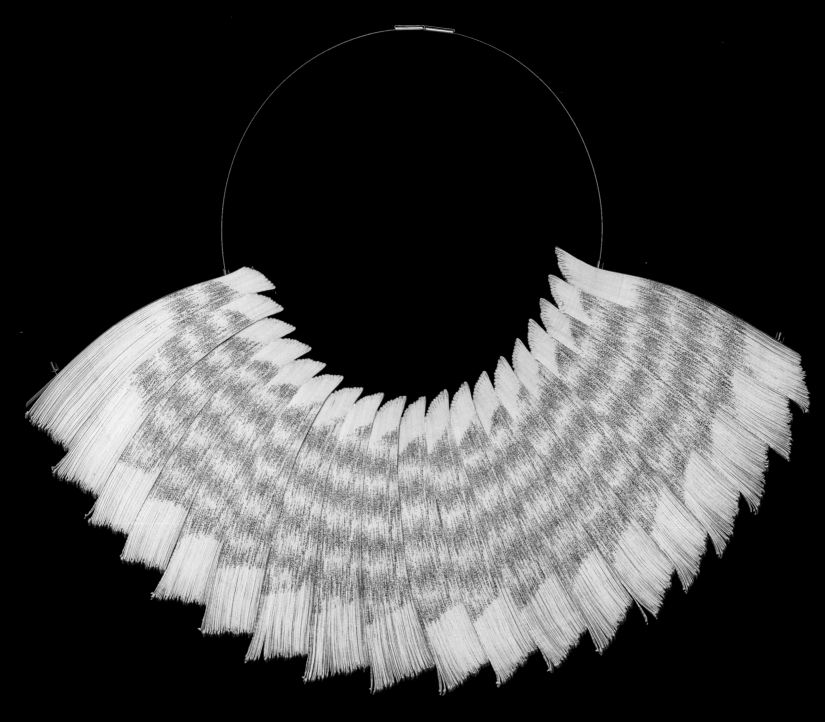

Linda MacNeil (United States, 1954–)
Necklace · 1995

Mirrored glass, gold
7 in. (17.8 cm), diameter
Gift of the artist, 2008

Kim Rawdin (United States, 1950–)
***How Many Wine Cups Have Stained This Moon with
the Songs of Old Friends...*** (bracelet) · c. 1997

Silver, gold, coral, lapis lazuli, sugolite, chalcedony
2 ¹/₄ x 3 ¹/₄ x 1 ³/₄ in. (5.7 x 8.3 x 4.4 cm)
Gift of Linda Schlenger, 2000

Alberto Zorzi (Italy, 1958–)
La Città (brooch) · 1997

Silver, lacquer
2 ¹/₂ x ¹/₂ in. (6.4 x 1.3 cm), diameter x depth
Gift of the artist, 2003

Richard H. Reinhardt (United States, 1921–1998)
Bracelet · **1993**

Silver
2 x 2 $^{1}/_{2}$ x 1 $^{1}/_{2}$ in. (5.1 x 6.4 x 3.8 cm)
Gift of Hope Byer, 2000

David Damkoehler (United States, 1943–)
T-1 (brooch) · **1993–95**

Stainless steel
2 $^{1}/_{2}$ x 14 $^{1}/_{2}$ x $^{1}/_{2}$ in. (6.4 x 36.8 x 1.3 cm)
Gift of Rosanne Raab, 1995

ROY, also known as **Rosemary Gialamas** (United States, 1962–)
Neopolis (brooch), closed and open · 1992

Silver
7 ³/₄ x 2 ¹⁵/₁₆ x ³/₈ in. (19.7 x 7.5 x 1 cm)
Gift of the artist in honor of her Greek immigrant grandparents, 1993

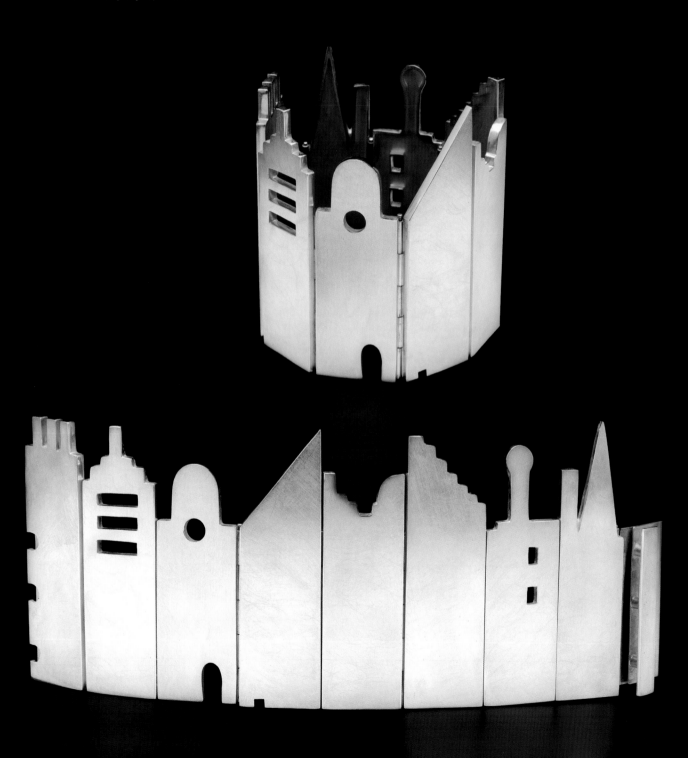

Richard Mawdsley (United States, 1945–)
Beta **(neckpiece) from the Architectural Series #2 · 1990–91**

Gold, pearls, lapis lazuli
14 ¹/₂ x 2 ³/₄ x 1 ⁵/₈ in. (36.8 x 7 x 4.1 cm)
Gift of an anonymous donor, 1995

Nancy Worden (United States, 1954–)
The Seven Deadly Sins (neckpiece), front · 1994

Silver, synthetic rubies, glass, found objects
8 ³⁄₄ x 8 ³⁄₄ x 1 in. (22.2 x 22.2 x 2.5 cm)
Gift of the artist and the William Traver Gallery, 1995

Nancy Worden (United States, 1954–)
The Seven Deadly Sins (neckpiece), back · 1994

Silver, synthetic rubies, glass, found objects
8 ³/₄ x 8 ³/₄ x 1 in. (22.2 x 22.2 x 2.5 cm)
Gift of the artist and the William Traver Gallery, 1995

Pat Flynn (United States, 1954–)
Heart Pins: Bound, Crumpled, Tied, Puzzled, Melted · c. 1999

Metal
1 ³/₄ x 1 ³/₄ x ⁵/₈ in. (4.4 x 4.4 x 1.6 cm), each
Gift of Suzan Marks, 1999

Ted Muehling (United States, 1953–)
Thorn Necklace · 1994

Silver
8 ¹/₂ x 8 x 2 in. (21.6 x 20.3 x 5.1 cm)
Gift of the artist, 1995

Kee-ho Yuen (China, 1956–current residence, United States)
Brooch · **1995**

Silver, bronze, enamel, laser printer ink, gold
2 ¹/₄ x 2 ¹/₄ x ¹/₂ in. (5.7 x 5.7 x 1.3 cm)
Gift of Chunghi Choo, 1998

Enid Kaplan (United States, 1954–2002, Israel)
The Nature of Personal Reality (neckpiece) · **1997**

Silver, bronze, copper, brass, wood, glass, aventurine, photograph, paint
15 ¹/₂ x 11 x 2 ¹/₄ in. (39.4 x 27.9 x 5.7 cm)
Gift of Dr. Eddi Lee, 1998

Jacqueline Lillie (France, 1941–current residence, Austria)
Fibula **(hairpiece) · 1990**

Glass beads, silver
7 7/8 x 3 9/16 in. (20 x 9 cm)
Promised gift of Barbara Tober, 2008

Joyce Scott (United States, 1948–)
Voices **(neckpiece) · 1993**

Glass beads, synthetic faceted discs, thread
12 3/4 x 11 3/4 x 1/2 in. (32.4 x 29.8 x 1.3 cm)
Museum purchase with funds provided by the Horace W. Goldsmith Foundation, 1994

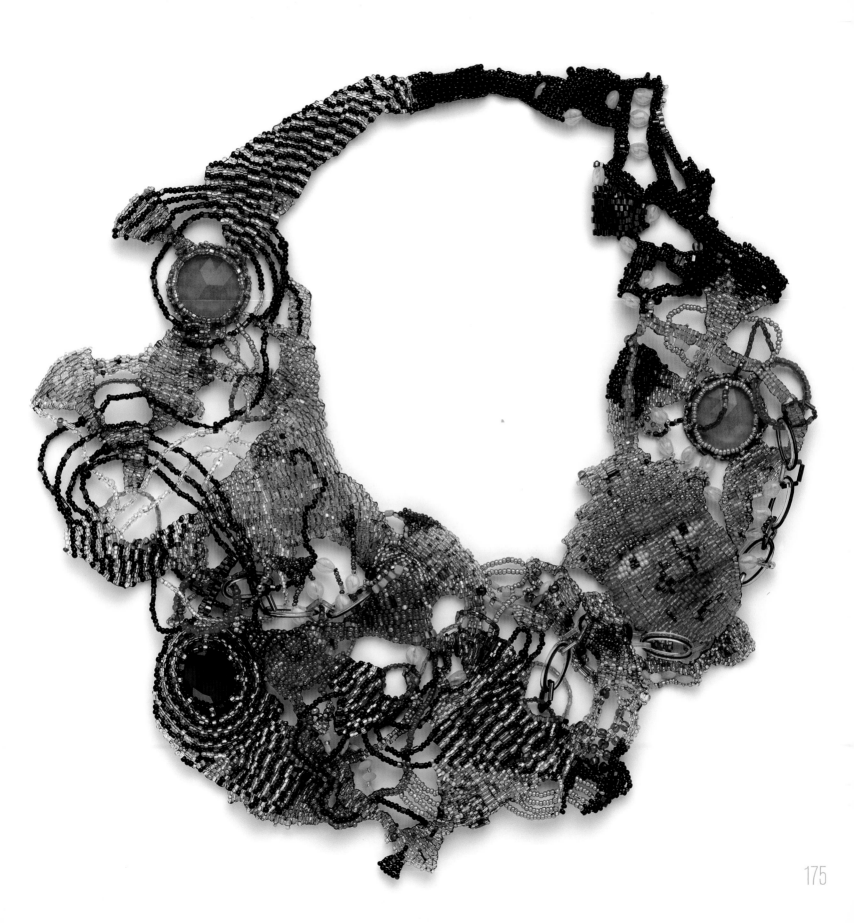

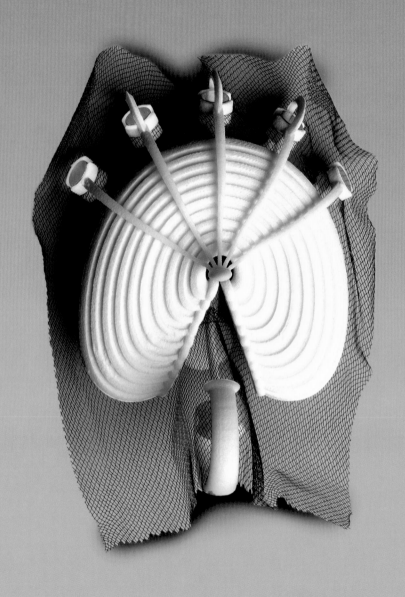

Daniella Kerner (Israel, 1952–current residence, United States)
Mag Brooch · **1999**

DuraForm polyamide, rare earth magnets
6 x 4 ¹/₂ x 2 ¹/₄ in. (15.2 x 11.4 x 5.7 cm)
Gift of Laura Anne Lechtzin, 2001

Stanley Lechtzin (United States, 1936–)
Plus-Minus Brooch · **1999**

Stereolithography, rapid-prototyped epoxy, rapid-prototyped gold
7 x 3 ¹/₄ x 1 ¹/₄ in. (17.8 x 8.3 x 3.2 cm)
Gift of Dr. Noah Lechtzin, 2001

Keith Lo Bue (United States, 1964–current residence, Australia)
The Sea Defeated (brooch) · 1993

Acrylic, silicone, cyanoacrylate, found objects
3 x 1 $^3/_4$ x $^3/_8$ in. (7.6 x 4.4 x 1 cm)
Gift of the artist, 1994

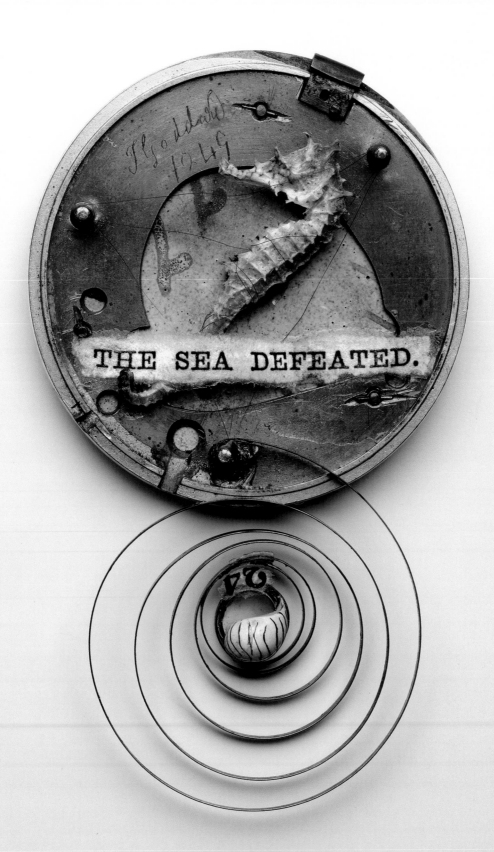

Stefano Marchetti	Robert Ellison, Jr.	Tina Rath
Peter Skubic	Rebecca Strzelec	Maria Phillips
Joan Ann Parcher	Kiwon Wang	John Iversen
Giovanni Corvaja	Dorothy Hogg	Liv Blåvarp
Mary Lee Hu	Lella Vignelli	Rami Abboud
Judy Kensley McKie	Ulla Kaufman	Karl Fritsch
Laurie J. Hall	Alyssa Dee Krauss	Giorgio Vigna
Sergey Jivetin	Dylan Poblano	Axel Russmeyer
Annamaria Zanella	Donald Friedlich	Bernd Munsteiner
Tamiko Kawata	Evert Nijland	Takashi Wada
Kiff Slemmons	Linda MacNeil	Ulrike Bahrs
Tone Vigeland	Sondra Sherman	Ted Noten
Tomoyo Hiraiwa	Enric Majoral	Boris Bally
Emiko Suo	Carrie Garrott	Michael Petry
Ruudt Peters	Jennifer Trask	

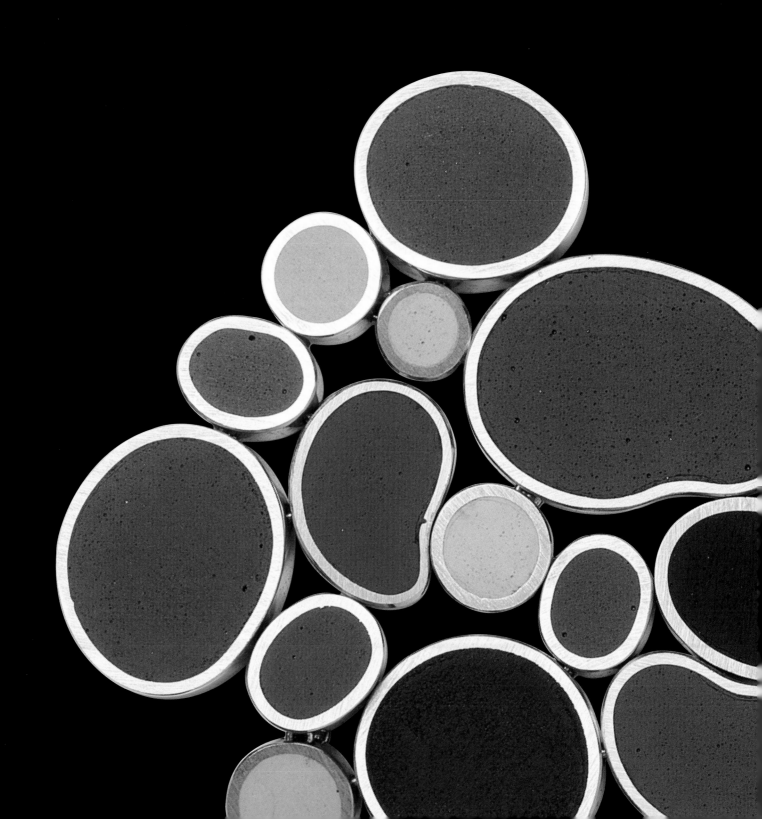

Stefano Marchetti (Italy, 1970–)
Bracelet · **2002**

Gold
3 ⅝ x 3 ⅝ x 2 in. (9.2 x 9.2 x 5.1 cm)
Gift of Dr. Neil H. Bander, 2003

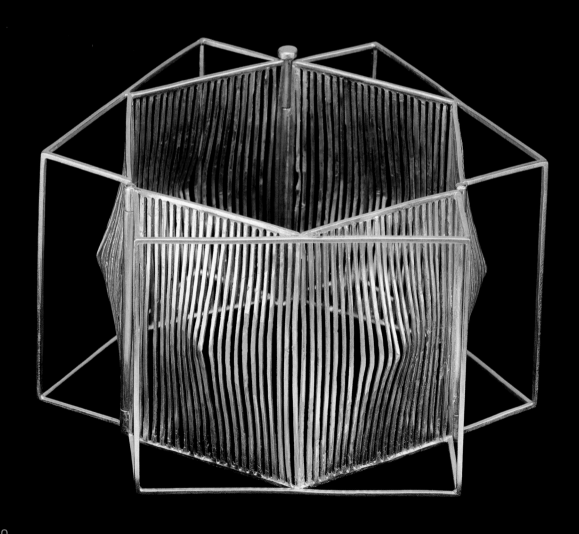

Peter Skubic (Yugoslavia, 1935–current residence, Austria)
Brooch · 2003

Stainless steel, lacquer, steel cable
5 ¹/₄ x 7 x 5 ¹/₄ in. (13.3 x 17.8 x 13.3 cm)
Museum purchase with funds provided by the Collections Committee, 2005

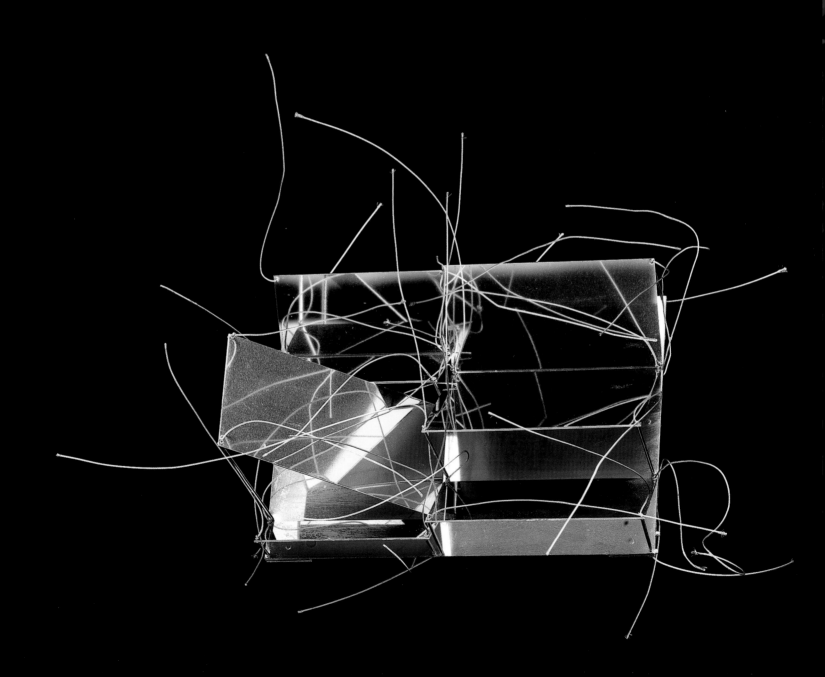

Joan Ann Parcher (United States, 1956–)
Brooch · **2002**

Glass, enamel, copper, silver
2 ³/₄ x 2 ³/₄ x ⁵/₈ in. (7 x 7 x 1.6 cm)
Museum purchase with funds provided by Ann Kaplan, 2002

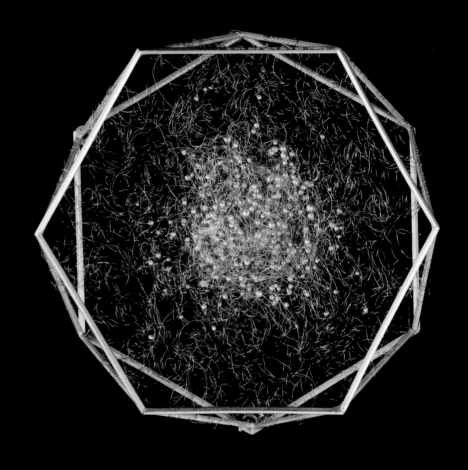

Giovanni Corvaja (Italy, 1971–)
Brooch · 2003

Gold, platinum wire
2 ³/₄ x 2 ³/₄ x ³/₄ in. (6 x 6 x 1.9 cm)
Promised gift of Aviva and Jack Robinson, 2006

Mary Lee Hu (United States, 1943–)
Bracelet #62 · 2002

Gold
2 $^{7}/_{8}$ x 3 $^{5}/_{8}$ x 2 $^{11}/_{16}$ in. (7.3 x 9.2 x 6.8 cm)
Museum purchase with funds provided by Ann Kaplan, 2002

Judy Kensley McKie (United States, 1944–)
Sidewinder Snake Bracelet · 2002

Gold, jadeite
2 ¹/₄ x 2 ³/₈ x 1 ¹/₂ in. (5.7 x 6 x 3.8 cm)
Promised gift of Barbara Tober, 2008

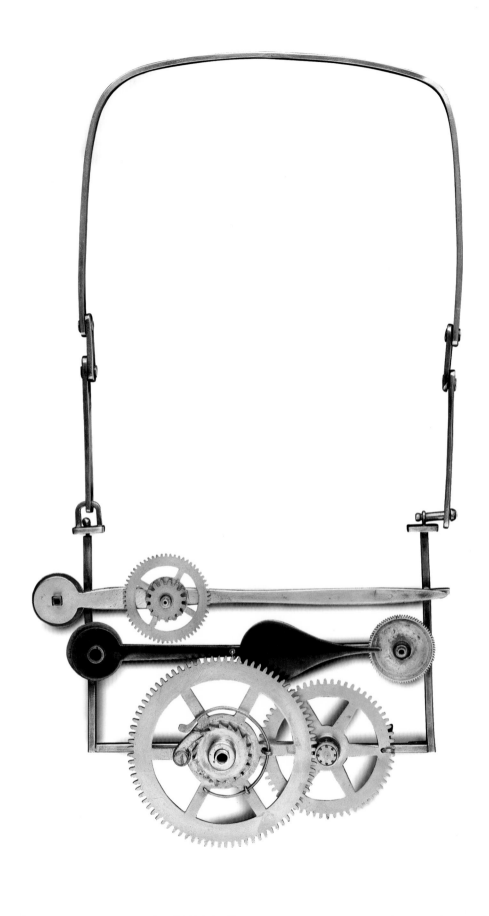

Laurie J. Hall (United States, 1944–)
It's About Time (neckpiece) · 2005

Silver, antique clock parts
11 x 6 x ¹/₄ in. (27.9 x 15.2 x 0.6 cm)
Promised gift of Mr. and Mrs. Lou Grotta, 2008

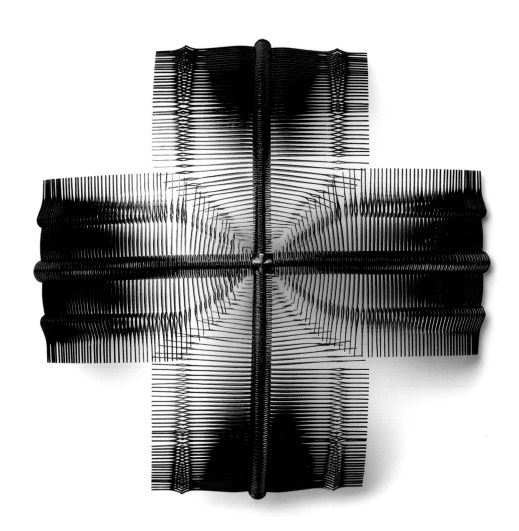

Sergey Jivetin (Uzbekistan, 1977–current residence, United States)
Intersection (brooch) · 2004

Watch hands, silver
3 ¹/₄ x 3 ¹/₄ x 1 in. (8.3 x 8.3 x 2.5 cm)
Museum purchase with funds provided by the Collections Committee, 2006

Annamaria Zanella (Italy, 1966–)
Building (brooch) · 2002

Silver, gold, enamel
3 x 2 ⁵/₈ x ³/₄ in. (7.6 x 6.7 x 1.9 cm)
Museum purchase with funds provided by the Horace W. Goldsmith Foundation, 2004

Tamiko Kawata (Japan, 1936–current residence, United States)
Black Orpheus (neckpiece) · 2006

Stainless steel safety pins, silver
9 ¹/₂ x 9 ¹/₂ x 1 ¹/₂ in. (24.1 x 24.1 x 3.8 cm)
Museum purchase with funds provided by LOOT! 2006
Purchase Committee and the Collections Committee, 2006

Kiff Slemmons (United States, 1944–)
Rattle Tags (necklace) · **2004**

Metal, paper
19 ¹/₂ in. (49.5 cm), length
Museum purchase with funds provided by LOOT! 2004 Purchase Committee, 2004

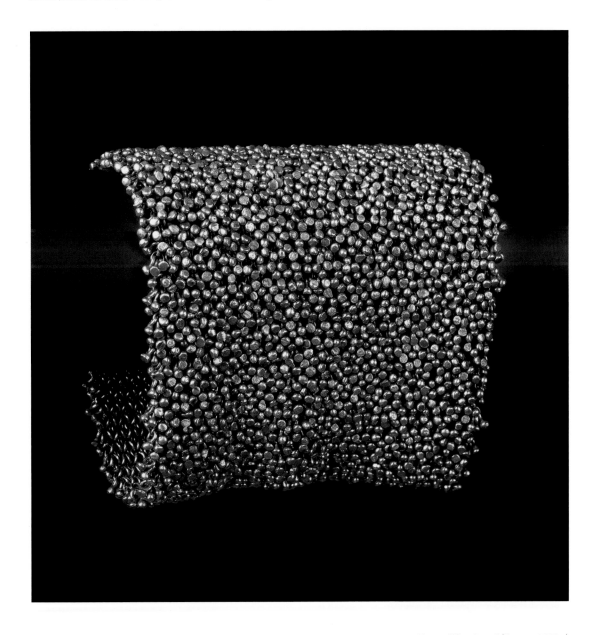

Tone Vigeland (Norway, 1938–)
Bracelet · **2000**

Steel
5 x 3 ¹/₄ in. (12.7 x 8.3 cm), length x diameter
Gift of Ambassador and Mrs. Edward E. Elson, 2000

Tomoyo Hiraiwa (Japan, 1948–)
Peace Wave #2 (brooch) · 2005

Silver, copper, *shakudo* (copper and gold alloy)
2 $^1/_2$ x 3 $^3/_8$ x 1 in. (6.4 x 8.6 x 2.5 cm)
Museum purchase with funds provided by Aviva and Jack Robinson, 2006

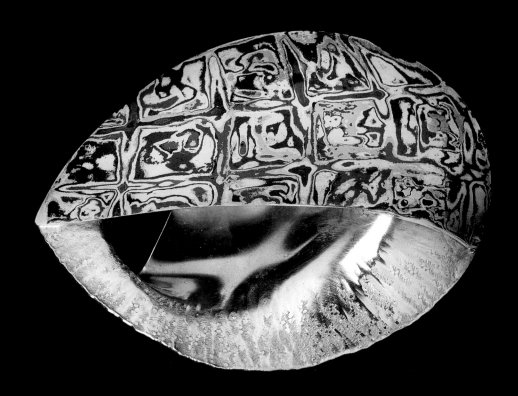

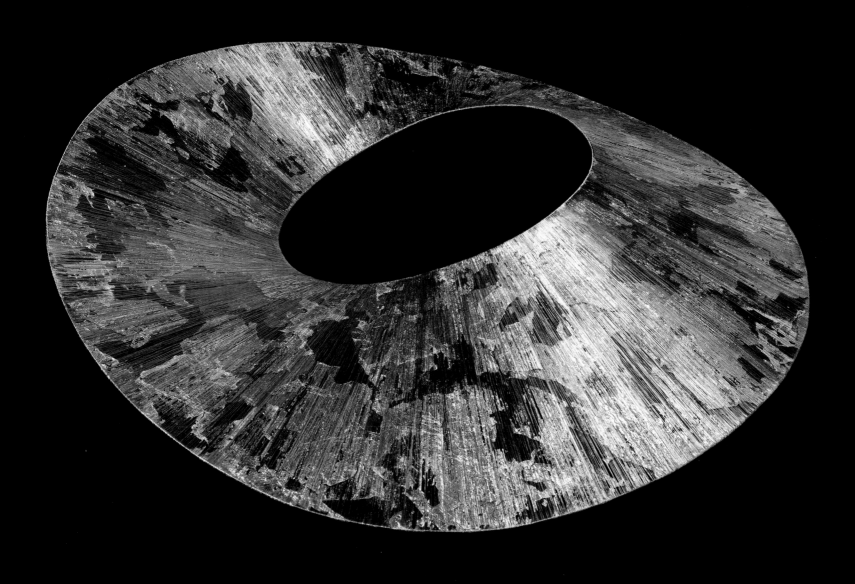

Emiko Suo (Japan, 1966–)
Collar · 2002

Stainless steel, gold leaf, silver leaf
18 x 18 ⅜ x 3 in. (45.7 x 46.7 x 7.6 cm)
Museum purchase with funds provided by Nanette L. Laitman, 2002

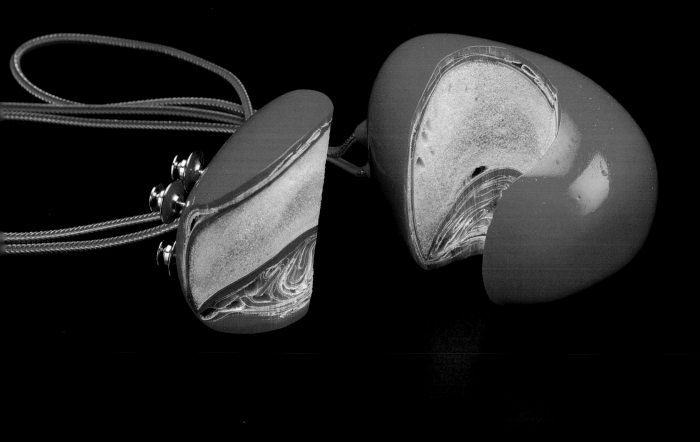

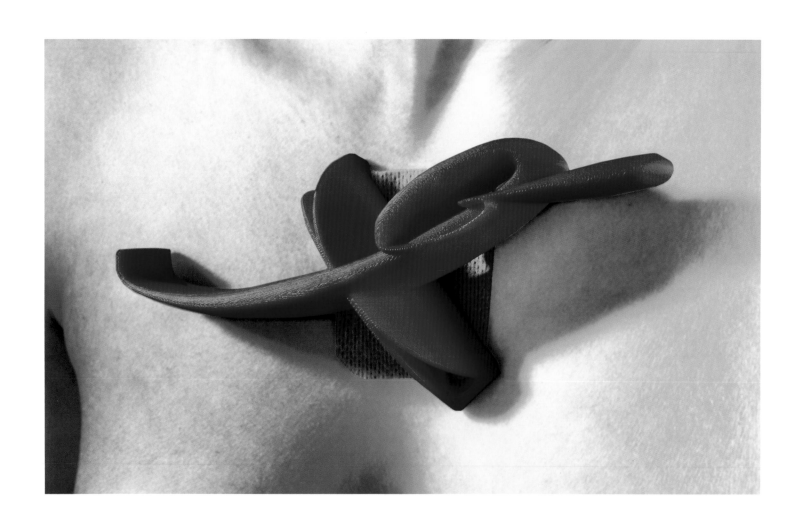

Rebecca Strzelec (United States, 1977–)
Line Brooch **from the Shorthand series · 2004**

ABS plastic (fused deposition modeled), medical adhesive
3 3/8 x 7 3/16 x 1 13/16 in. (8.6 x 18.3 x 4.6 cm)
Gift of the artist in honor of Dale and Donna Strzelec, 2008

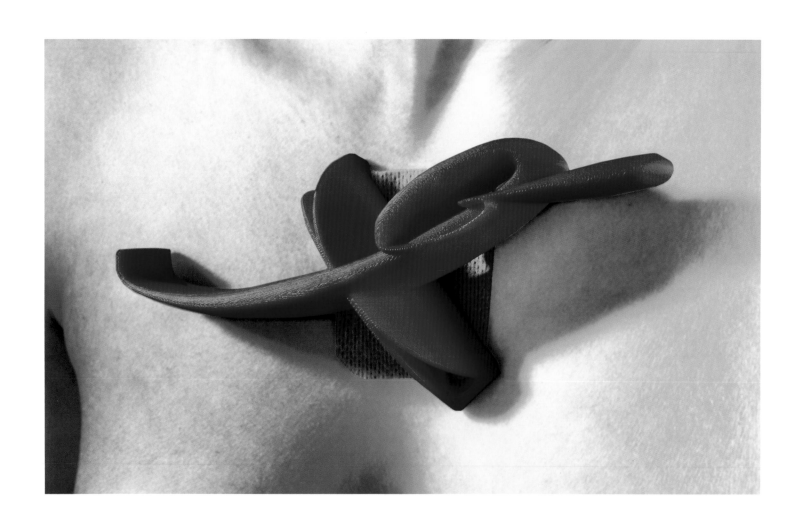

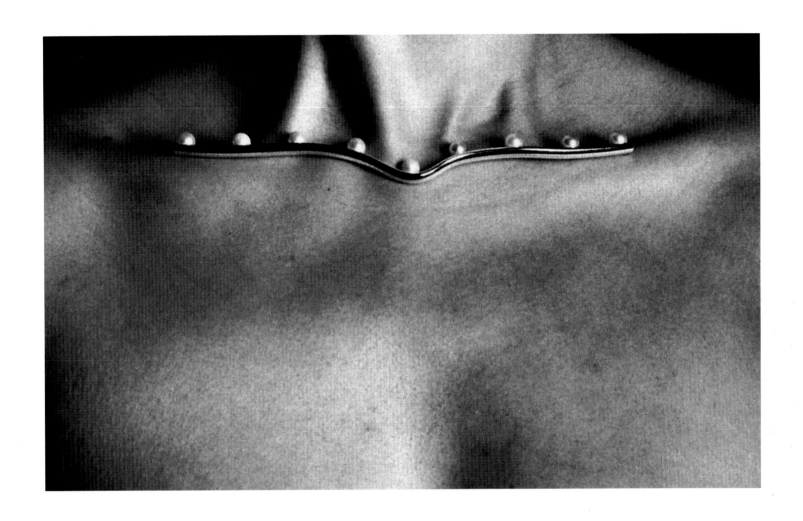

Kiwon Wang (Korea, 1962–current residence, United States)
Neckpiece · **2008**

Silver, pearls, monofilament
5 x 7 ¹/₂ x ⁵/₁₆ in. (12.7 x 19.1 x 0.8 cm)
Gift of the artist, 2008

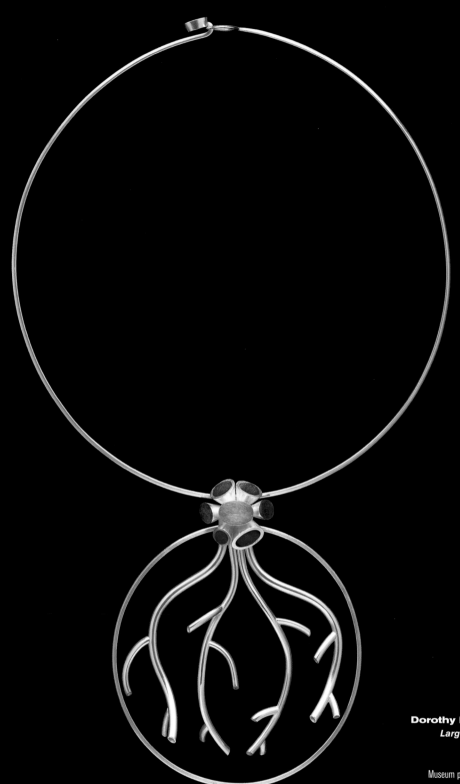

Dorothy Hogg (Scotland, 1945–current residence, England)
Large Circle Neckpiece **from the Artery series · 2005**

Silver, felt
12 x 7 ¹/₄ x ³/₄ in. (30.5 x 18.4 x 1.9 cm)
Museum purchase with funds provided by LOOT! 2006 Purchase Committee
and the Collections Committee, 2006

Kiff Slemmons (United States, 1944–)
Circumspect (neckpiece) · 2003

Silver, brass, mirrors, lenses
14 x 13 x $\frac{1}{2}$ in. (35.6 x 33 x 1.3 cm)
Museum purchase with funds provided by Ann Kaplan, 2004

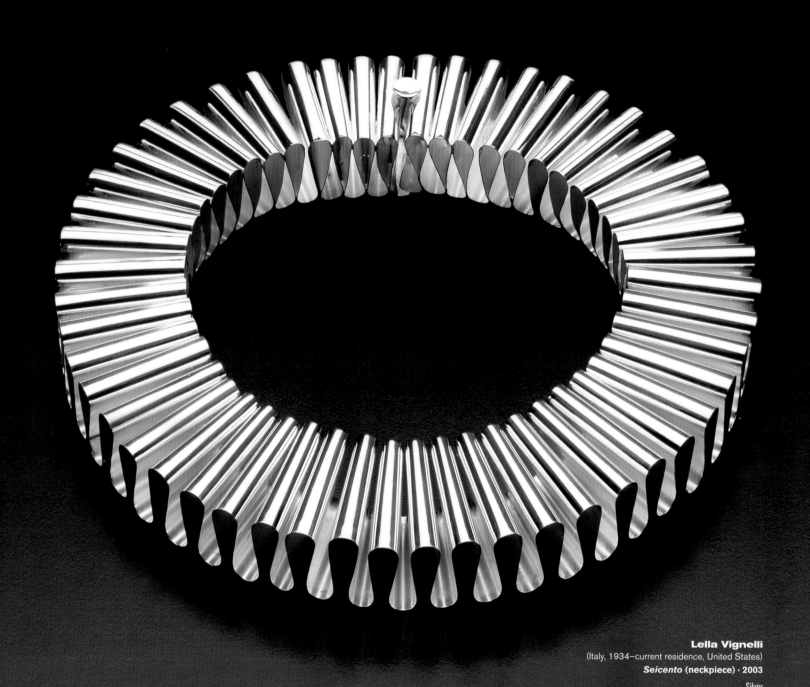

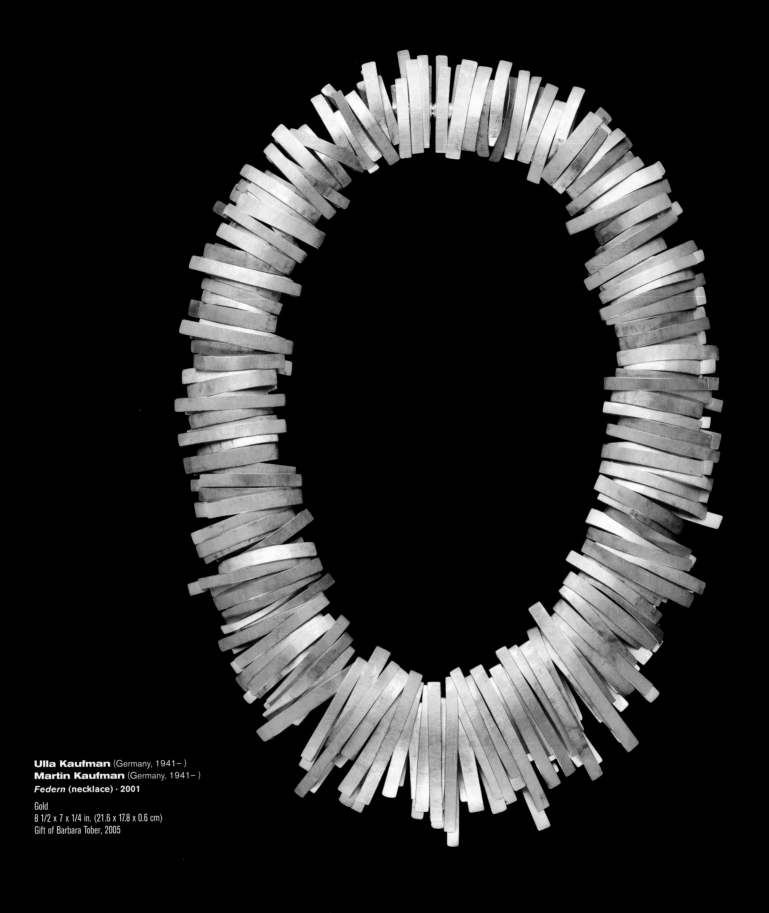

Ulla Kaufman (Germany, 1941–)
Martin Kaufman (Germany, 1941–)
Federn (necklace) · 2001

Gold
8 1/2 x 7 x 1/4 in. (21.6 x 17.8 x 0.6 cm)
Gift of Barbara Tober, 2005

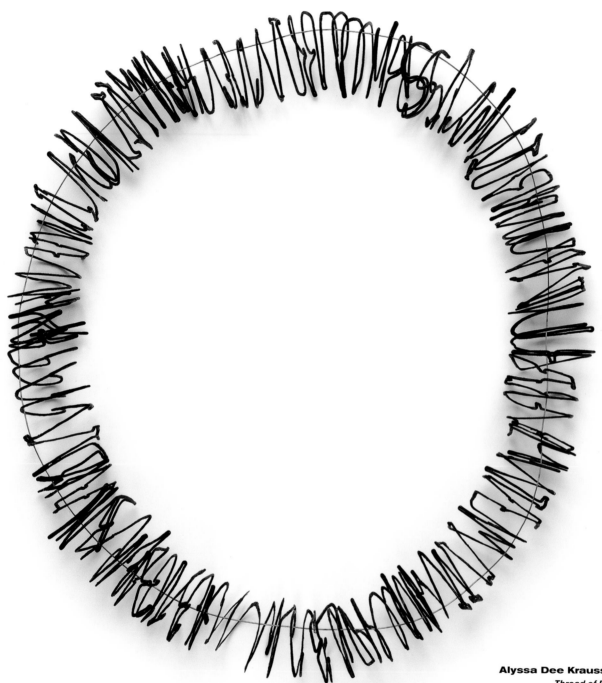

Alyssa Dee Krauss (United States, 1962–)
Thread of Faith (neckpiece) · **2000**

Iron, gold
10 ¹/₂ x 8 ¹/₂ x ¹/₂ in. (26.7 x 21.6 x 1.3 cm)
Museum purchase with funds provided by LOOT! 2000 Purchase Committee, 2000

Kiff Slemmons (United States, 1944–)
Nibs (necklace) · 2000

Silver, ebony, mica, manuscript fragments
16 ¹/₂ in. (41.9 cm), length
Promised gift of Marcia Docter, 2008

Dylan Poblano (United States, 1974–)
Mondrian Stackable Ring · 2001

Silver, turquoise, quartz
1 3/4 x 1 1/8 x 1 1/4 in. (4.4 x 2.9 x 3.2 cm)
Gift of the artist, 2004

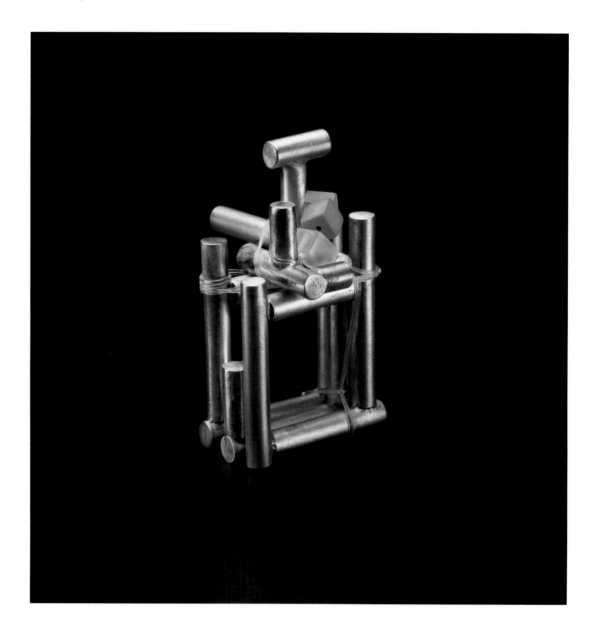

Dylan Poblano (United States, 1974–)
21st-century Neckpiece · 2001

Silver, quartz
12 1/2 x 6 x 1 1/2 in. (31.8 x 15.2 x 3.8 cm)
Gift of the artist, 2004

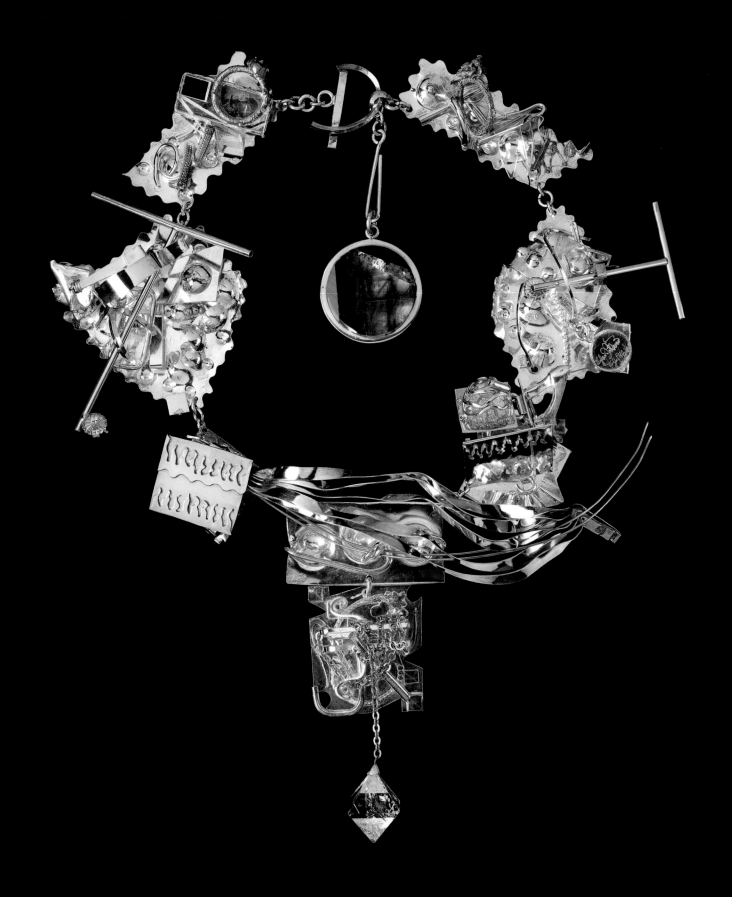

Donald Friedlich (United States, 1954–)
Magnification Series Brooch · 2008

Glass, gold
3 x 2 ³/₄ x ¹/₂ in. (7.6 x 7 x 1.3 cm)
Gift of the artist, 2008

Evert Nijland (The Netherlands, 1971–)
Fiori (necklace) from the Venezia series · 2006

Flameworked glass, glass beads, silk thread, gold
7 ¹/₂ x ¹/₂ in. (19.1 x 1.3 cm), diameter x depth
Museum purchase with funds provided by Susan Grant Lewin, 2007

Sondra Sherman (United States, 1958–)
Corsage: Papaver Somniferum-Poppy · **2007**

Steel, nail polish
4 x 2 ³/₄ x 1 in. (10.2 x 7 x 2.5 cm)
Museum purchase with funds provided by Marcia Docter, 2008

Enric Majoral (Spain, 1949–)
Brooch VVA230 from the Joies de Sorra [Sand Jewels]
collection · 2006
Oxidized silver, acrylic paint
2 ³/₄ x 1 ³/₈ x ³/₁₆ in. (7 x 3.5 x 0.5 cm)
Gift of the artist and Aaron Faber Gallery, 2007

Enric Majoral (Spain, 1949–)
Ring VVAA40 from the Joies de Sorra [Sand Jewels]
collection · 2006

Oxidized silver, acrylic paint
2 3/16 x 1 3/4 in. (5.5 x 4.5 cm)
Gift of the artist and Aaron Faber Gallery, 2007

Carrie Garrott (United States, 1974–)
Cluster Brooches · 2004

Wax, silver, rose petals
1 ¹/₂ in. (3.8 cm), approximate diameter
Museum purchase with funds provided by the Collections Committee, 2006

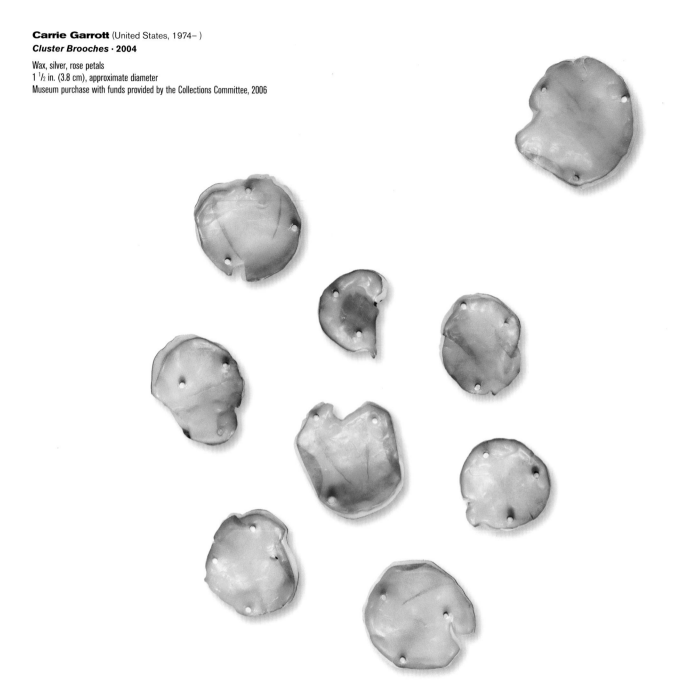

Jennifer Trask (United States, 1970–)
Blue/Black Necklace · 2003

Gold, silver, lead, morpho butterfly wings, leaf beetle (Chrysomelidae),
iron, pigments, rutile, ilmenite, charcoal, Ulysses butterfly (Papilio ulysses),
peacock (Pavo) feathers
7 ³/₄ x 6 ¹/₄ x ¹/₄ in. (19.7 x 15.9 x 0.6 cm)
Museum purchase with funds provided by LOOT! 2004 Purchase Committee, 2004

215

Tina Rath (United States, 1968–)
Belgian Floral Collar · 2000

Silver, ebony, stainless steel, paint
9 x 9 x 1 ³/₈ in. (22.9 x 22.9 x 3.5 cm)
Gift of Barbara Tober, 2001

Maria Phillips (United States, 1963–)
Swell (neckpiece) · 2005

Pig gut, steel, thread, beads, silver
11 ¹/₂ x 11 x 2 in. (29.2 x 27.9 x 5.1 cm)
Museum purchase with funds provided by the Collections Committee, 2005

216

John Iversen (Germany, 1953–current residence, United States)
Bracelet · 2002

Gold, enamel
6 ¹/₂ x 1 ³/₄ x ³/₁₆ in. (16.5 x 4.4 x 0.5 cm)
Museum purchase with funds provided by Ann Kaplan, 2002

Liv Blåvarp (Norway, 1956–)
Necklace · 2002

Dyed sycamore, painted birch, gold leaf
11 x 8 x 2 in. (27.9 x 20.3 x 5.1 cm)
Gift of Barbara Tober, 2002

Rami Abboud (Lebanon, 1960 – current residence, France and Lebanon)
Omnipotent (ring) · 2007

Gold, topaz, tourmalines, sapphires, diamonds
1 ⁵/₈ x 1 ¹/₄ x 2 in. (4.1 x 3.2 x 5.1 cm)
Gift of the artist in honor of Barbara Tober, 2008

Karl Fritsch (Germany, 1963–)
Ring · 2006

Gold, diamonds
2 3/8 x 7/8 x 3/8 in. (6 x 2.2 x 1 cm)
Promised gift of Susan Grant Lewin, 2008

Giorgio Vigna (Italy, 1955–)
Gorgoglio (neckpiece) · 2002

Blown glass, copper, silver
15 ³/₄ x 6 in. (40 x 15.2 cm)
Gift of the artist, 2008

Axel Russmeyer (Germany, 1964–)
Necklace · 2002

Glass beads, resin, ribbon, gold, thread
18 x 1 ³/₁₆ in. (45.7 x 3 cm), diameter x depth
Gift of the artist, 2004

Bernd Munsteiner (Germany, 1943–)
Brooch/Pendant · **c. 2001**

Lapis lazuli, aquamarine, gold
2 7/8 x 1 7/8 in. (7.3 x 4.8 cm)
Gift of the artist, 2002

Takashi Wada (Japan, 1938–current residence, United States)
Brooch · 2002

Silver, lapis lazuli
3 $^3/_8$ x 3 $^3/_8$ x $^1/_2$ in. (8.6 x 8.6 x 1.3cm)
Museum purchase with funds provided by Ann Kaplan, 2002

Ulrike Bahrs (Germany, 1944–)
Brooch · **c. 2000**

Gold, silver, garnets, hologram
3 x 2 7/8 x 3/8 in. (7.6 x 7.3 x 1 cm)
Museum purchase with funds provided by LOOT! 2000 Purchase Committee, 2000

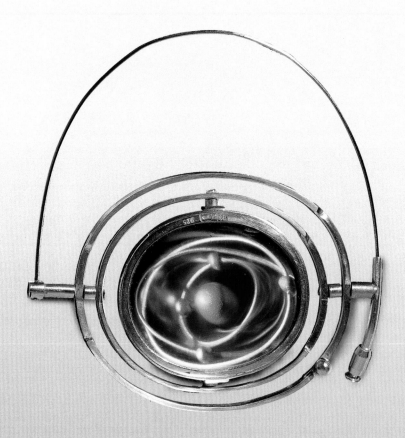

Ted Noten (The Netherlands, 1956–)
Siberian Necklace #1 · *2007*

Gold, birch wood, grasshoppers, housefly with diamond, synthetic ruby,
Christoffel Medallion, cultured pearls
31 in. (78.7 cm), length
Promised gift of Marcia Docter, 2008

Boris Bally (United States, 1961–)
Untitled Drawing · 1999

Paper, ink, pencil
10 ⁷/₈ x 14 in. (27.6 x 35.6 cm)
Gift of the artist, 2006

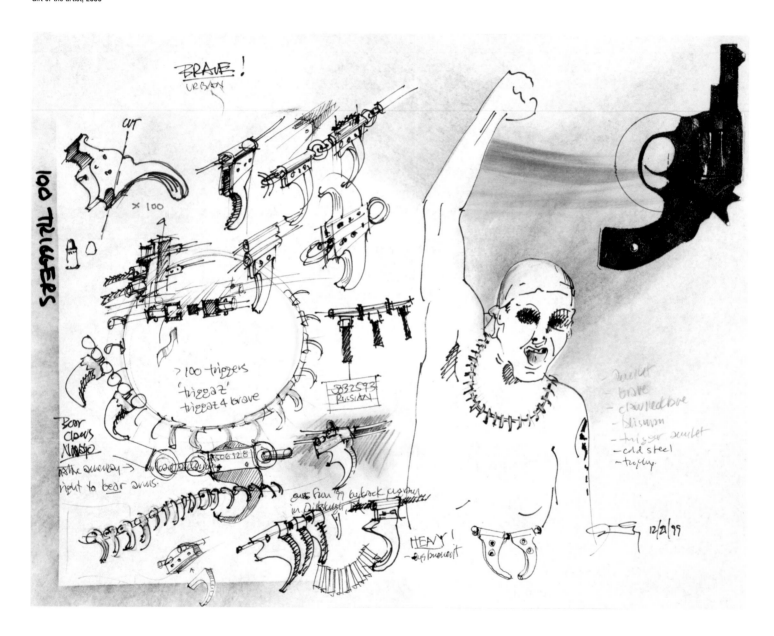

Boris Bally (United States, 1961–)
Brave #2 (neckpiece) · 2006

Found steel handgun triggers, gold, white sapphire, silver, steel cable
24 ¹/₂ x 12 x 1 ¹/₈ in. (62.2 x 30.5 x 2.9 cm)
Gift of the artist in honor of Alex Schaffner, Basel, Switzerland, 2006

Michael Petry (United States, 1960–current residence, England)
The Treasure of Memory · 2000

Blown glass, yachting rope
600 in. (1524 cm), length
Gift of Devin Borden and Hiram Butler, 2007

ARTISTS in the Jewelry Collection

Rami Abboud
Ita Aber
Constance Abernathy
Deborah Aguado
Marcus Amerman
Galia Amsel
Joe Reyes Apodaca
Glenda Arentzen
Lily Asher
Ulrike Bahrs
Gijs Bakker
Boris Bally
Julia Barello
Ela Bauer
J. Begay
Jamie Bennett
Claire Bersani
Mike Bird-Romero
Liv Blåvarp
Flora Book
Michael Brandt
Ed Brickman
Caroline Broadhead
Lola Brooks
Irena Brynner
Bussi Buhs
Vivianna Torun Bülow-Hübe
Pierre Cavalan
Peter Chang
Claude Chavent
Françoise Chavent
Sharon Church
Colette
Betty Cooke
Giovanni Corvaja
Ken Cory
Paolo Costagli
Margret Craver
Cara Croninger
Angela Cummings
Ramón Puig Cuyàs
David Damkoehler
Bartow G. Daniels

Rian de Jong
Margaret De Patta
Lam de Wolf
Michele Oka Doner
Marilyn Druin
Robert W. Ebendorf
Alma Eikerman
Eva Eisler
Robert Ellison Jr.
Barbara Engle
Sandra Enterline
Claire Falkenstein
Phillip Fike
Anne Finlay
Arline M. Fisch
Pat Flynn
Nora Fok
David Freda
Elsa Freund
Donald Friedlich
Karl Fritsch
Carrie Garrott
David Gaussoin
Frank Gehry
Thomas Gentille
Imogene Bailey Gieling
Kathryn Regier Gough
Gabrielle Gould
Lisa Gralnick
Stanislava Grebení ková
William Perry Griffiths
Marie Aimee Grimaldi
Red Grooms
Laurie J. Hall
Susan Hamlet
William Harper
Susanna Heron
Yu Hiraishi
Tomoyo Hiraiwa
Dorothy Hogg
Tina Fung Holder
Mary Lee Hu
Alice Hutchins

John Iversen
Bob Jefferson
Georg Jensen
Kaarin Bonde Jensen
Michael John Jerry
Sergey Jivetin
Daniel Jocz
Svenja John
Darrell Jumbo
Hermann Jünger
Enid Kaplan
Gertrude Karlan
Alfred Karram
Judith Kaufman
Martin Kaufman
Ulla Kaufman
Tamiko Kawata
Daniella Kerner
Sung Ran Kim
Alice Klein
Esther Knobel
Henning Koppel
Sam Kramer
Alyssa Dee Krauss
Mary Kretsinger
Shana Kroiz
Otto Künzli
Michael Lacktman
Kenneth Jay Lane
Ibram Lassaw
Stanley Lechtzin
Jacqueline Lillie
Keith Lo Bue
Paul A. Lobel
Ken Loeber
Charles Loloma
Randy J. Long
Diane Love
Linda MacNeil
Enric Majoral
Julia Manheim
Thomas Mann
K. Lee Manuel

Stefano Marchetti
Bill Martin
Bruno Martinazzi
Wilhelm Tasso Mattar
Richard Mawdsley
Mary McFadden
Judy Kensley McKie
Bruce Metcalf
Giuliana Michelotti
Julie Anne Mihalisin
John Paul Miller
Myra Mimlitsch-Gray
Norman Mizuno
Mascha Moje
Robert Lee Morris
Ted Muehling
Bernd Munsteiner
Tom Munsteiner
Evert Nijland
Ruth Nivola
Ted Noten
Pavel Opočenský
Joan Ann Parcher
Earl Pardon
Tod Pardon
Rowena Park
Barbara Patrick
Zack Peabody
Ronald Hayes Pearson
Lee Barnes Peck
Jo Pedersen
Susana Pesce
Norbert Peshlakai
Ruudt Peters
Michael Petry
Maria Phillips
Gene Pijanowski
Dylan Poblano
Jovanna Poblano
Veronica Poblano

Charlotte Pols
Gio Pomodoro
Irving Potter
Gretchen Raber
Ruth Radakovich
Svetozar Radakovich
Wendy Ramshaw
Tina Rath
Kim Rawdin
Vernon Reed
Henry Reim Vis
Richard H. Reinhardt
Merry Renk
Ruth Schirmer Roach
Alida Rudjord Roiseland
Jessica Rose
Ivy Ross
Gerd Rothmann
ROY
Eduardo Rubio-Arzate
Axel Russmeyer
Claire Sanford
Hiroko Sato-Pijanowski
Gayle Saunders
Mary Ann Scherr
Marjorie Schick
Joyce Scott
Ronald Senungetuk
Alice Shannon
Sondra Sherman
Verena Sieber-Fuchs
Olaf Skoogfors
Peter Skubic
Louise Slater
Kiff Slemmons
Arthur Smith
Christina Smith
Ramona Solberg
Lisa Spiros
Marianne Spottswood

Missy Stevens
Rebecca Strzelec
Barbara Stutman
Emiko Suo
Charles Supplee
Sandy Swirnoff
Janna Syvänoja
Billie Jean Theide
Rachelle Thiewes
Linda Threadgill
David Tisdale
Jennifer Trask
Ray Urban
Emmy van Leersum
Tone Vigeland
Giorgio Vigna
Lella Vignelli
Pier Voulkos
Takashi Wada
Denise Wallace
Kiwon Wang
David Watkins
Lynda Watson-Abbott
David Webb
Efrem Weitzman
Heather White van Stolk
Ed Wiener
Rodney M. Winfield
Bob Winston
Jeff Wise
Susan Wise
Barbara Natoli Witt
J. Fred Woell
Beatrice Wood
Nancy Worden
Kee-ho Yuen
Annamaria Zanella
Marci Zelmanoff
Michael Zobel
Alberto Zorzi

DONORS to the Jewelry Collection

Aaron Faber Gallery
Joshua Aber
Allied Craftsmen of San Diego
American Craft Council
Artium Ltd.
Neil H. Bander
Barbara Rockefeller Foundation
Barry Friedman Ltd.
Joan Baxt
Beatrice Wood Foundation
Edna S. Beron
Eleanor Bersani
Allison Bird-Romero
Helen Bock
Cliff Booth
Romala and Dan Booton
Devin Borden and Hiram Butler
Hope Byer
Michele Caplan
Chunghi Choo
Garth Clark and Mark Del Vecchio
Herbert Coyne
Margo Cutler
Mr. and Mrs. Bartow V. Daniels
Alan J. Davidson
Estate of Margaret De Patta and
   Eugene Bielawski
Marcia Docter
Mel Druin, Allison Druin, Erica
   Druin, and Laura Druin Griffin
Dr. and Mrs. Alberto Eiber
Helen Williams Drutt English
Ambassador and Mrs. Edward E.
   Elson
Daphne and Peter Farago
Nina D. Fieldsteel
Drs. Lois A. and Robert E. Fisch
Natalie and Greg Fitz-Gerald
Elaine Galinson
Robert and Rae Gilson
The Horace W. Goldsmith
   Foundation
Dorothy Twining Globus

Lorna Hyde Graev
Sandy Grotta
Amy Hanan
Jane Hershey
Historical Design, Inc.
   Dennis Gallion
   Daniel Morris
Virginia Holshuh
Holly Hotchner
Mary Lee Hu
Johnson Wax Company
Wendy Evans Joseph
Ann Kaplan
Janet Kardon
Diane and Joel Karp
Jane Korman
Nanette L. Laitman
Edith Lechtzin
Laura Anne Lechtzin
Dr. Noah Lechtzin
Dr. Eddi Lee
Lynn and Jeffrey Leff
Susan Grant Lewin
Mimi S. Livingston
Mildred Loew
Sonia and Isaac Luski
Joanne Lyman
Nancy and Edwin Marks
Suzan Marks
Vivian and Edward Merrin
Mobilia Gallery
Museum of Arts and Design
   Collections Committee
Museum of Arts and Design
   LOOT! 2000 Purchase
   Committee
Museum of Arts and Design
   LOOT! 2004 Purchase
   Committee
Museum of Arts and Design
   LOOT! 2006 Purchase
   Committee
Serga and Daniel Nadler

Dr. and Mrs. Malcolm A. Nanes
National Endowment for the Arts
Ursula Ilse-Neuman
James Nicholas
Wyatt Osato
Laura Selwyn Oskowitz
Patricia Pastor
Anne W. Potter
Rosanne Raab
Christianna Irene and Kurt
   Christian Raber
Toza Radakovich
Mr. and Mrs. Edward Riegelhaupt
Chris Rifkin
Aviva and Jack Robinson
Pat Rodimer
Joanna Roos
Estate of Jessica Rose
Eleanor T. and Samuel J.
   Rosenfeld
The Rotasa Trust Collection
Dr. and Mrs. Isidore Samuels
Dr. James B. M. Schick, Robert M.
   Schick, and Mrs. Eleanor Krask
Linda Schlenger
Peter Schmid
Donna Schneier
Stanley Seidman
Irene Shapiro and Rosalyn
   Copleman
Stuart Ross Smith
Ida Crawford Stewart
Betty Tarnoff
Tiffany & Co. Foundation
Barbara Tober
Bettianne Welch
William Traver Gallery
Armand Winfield
Paul Wittenborn
Marci Zelmanoff
Ann Ziff